SPIRIT LIKE A STORM
The Story of Mary Shelley

World Writers

SPIRIT LIKE A STORM
The Story of Mary Shelley

Calvin Craig Miller

MORGAN
REYNOLDS
Incorporated

Greensboro

SPIRIT LIKE A STORM *The Story of Mary Shelley*

Copyright © 1996 by Calvin Craig Miller

Library of Congress Cataloging-in-Publication Data
Miller, Calvin Craig, 1954-
   Spirit like a storm : the story of Mary Shelley / Calvin Craig Miller.
      p. cm. -- (World Writers)
   Includes bibliographical references and index.
   Summary: A biography of the nineteenth-century English author who at the age of
   nineteen wrote the classic horror novel, "Frankenstein."
   ISBN 1-883846-13-7
      1. Shelley, Mary Wollstonecraft, 1797-1851--Biography—Juvenile literature.
2. Women authors, English--19th century--Biography--Juvenile literature.   [1. Shelley,
Mary Wollstonecraft, 1797-1851. 2. Authors, English. 3. Women--Biography.]   I. Title
II. Series
PR5398.M5 1996
823'.7—dc20
[B]

                                                                                    95-53826
                                                                                    CIP
                                                                                    AC

Printed in the United States of America
First Edition

To
Virginia Ruth Bare

CONTENTS

The Mother Gone Before

Most young women would have found Mary Godwin's home on Skinner Street in London to be a far more inviting place than the graveyard at St. Pancras Church. But Mary preferred spending time at the cemetery, where she could be overheard speaking aloud to the spirit of her departed mother. Sometimes she stayed after dark, falling asleep on Mary Wollstonecraft's grave.

Although Wollstonecraft died while giving birth to her daughter in 1787, her ideas, as set out in her book *A Vindication of the Rights of Women,* had been the cause of many heated arguments throughout Great Britain, and deeply influenced young Mary Godwin's life.

Mary Wollstonecraft argued forcefully that men and women should be equal, with the same access to education and the same legal protections. Marriage should be an equal partnership, instead of the man having legal control of his wife and property as the law then stated. But most shocking of all, Mary Wollstonecraft said that marriage was not necessary to raise children, nor was it morally wrong to bear children out of wedlock.

Her writings made the beautiful Mary Wollstonecraft famous. But she did more than write about her ideas—she tried to live them. When she had met the American Gilbert Imlay, fell in love, and bore a daughter she named Fanny out of wedlock, Mary proved she was willing to put her philosophy into practice. But then Imlay deserted her and Fanny. Mary, overcome with despair, attempted to commit suicide by jumping into the Thames River.

It was at this low-point in her life that Mary Wollstonecraft met William Godwin. Godwin was also a radical writer who attacked all current forms of government as well as the Christian church. His book *Political Justice* was so popular among some intellectuals that it became the center of a new movement in literature, art, and philosophy that was then flourishing in Great Britain. Godwin argued that individual freedom was the primary purpose of life, and that freedom could only be found outside the constraints of society. Free love, for example, was more "natural" than marriage. Therefore the institution of marriage should be eliminated.

Considering their philosophies, there was great surprise when Mary Wollstonecraft and William Godwin were married on March 29, 1797 in St. Pancras Church. Here were the two advocates of free love, who both believed religion was one of the enemies of individual freedom, being married in a church! But sometimes life interferes with philosophy, and what their followers didn't know was that Wollstonecraft was pregnant and she knew from bitter experience how society treated the children of unwed mothers. Both she and Godwin wanted better

This portrait of Mary Wollstonecraft was painted when she lived in Paris

treatment for their child. After the wedding, they settled into domestic life at Godwin's house on Skinner Street.

But their married life was to be short-lived. Wollstonecraft went into labor on August 29. Almost immediately, there were complications that continued after the birth of the baby girl. Wollstonecraft lingered in an agonized daze for twelve days until she died on the morning of September 10. Five months after her wedding, she was buried in the graveyard of St. Pancras Church. Godwin had a gravestone raised that declared her greatest accomplishment:

Mary Wollstonecraft Godwin
Author of
A Vindication of the Rights of Women

The baby was given her mother's name and the little girl filled the usually aloof Godwin with fatherly tenderness. "She shall be nobody's little girl but papa's" Godwin wrote once, while traveling in Ireland on business.

Many of the people who had adopted Mary Wollstonecraft's ideas visited the Godwin home during Mary Godwin's childhood. Their memories kept her unknown mother alive, and, at an early age, little Mary decided to live her life outside the conventions of society. Convinced she was born to greatness, Mary felt both the freedom and the burden of that legacy. The trips to the grave gave her a chance to commune with her mother's spirit.

There was another, less romantic, reason for Mary's trips to St. Pancras. Godwin remarried when she was three and her stepmother, who was also named Mary, was a much different woman than the first Mrs. Godwin. Practical minded, especially in money matters, rather plain, with a tendency toward plumpness, Mary Jane Godwin had to endure unflattering comparisons to the beautiful and intelligent first wife. She particularly hated the fact Mary was Godwin's favorite child. This resentment grew after she and Godwin had a son, William. She also resented the way her children, Jane and Charles Clairmont, were overshadowed by Mary.

The new Mrs. Godwin also rejected Mary Wollstoncraft's

philosophy. To young Mary her mother's ideas were beyond criticism. This difference of opinion doomed any chance the two would ever reconcile.

Despite the conflicts, all was not miserable in the comfortable, five-story house. The ground floor was occupied by the family's publishing company, M.J. Godwin and Co. The company published children's books and the carved head of Aesop, a legendary teller of fables, looked out over a curved display window. Above the office and book shop the top four floors provided spacious family living quarters, although the parlor was often crowded by the stream of Godwin's admirers and visitors. Mary, her half-sister Fanny and stepsister Jane—"the Goddesses," as Godwin playfully called them—had a floor to themselves, equipped with a school room, where they studied with a governess. Although Mary was assigned chores, she also enjoyed a great deal of independence, taking meals, entertaining friends, reading, and spinning daydreams that cast her as a romantic heroine.

Jane Clairmont, Mary's stepsister, who later changed her name to Claire because she felt Claire Clairmont had a more musical air, grew into a bright, high-spirited young woman, gifted with a sense of humor and a lovely singing voice. Her gaiety could be contagious, although her mood could shift suddenly to depression and anger. Claire could never get enough of the spotlight, singing mischievous songs and mimicking Godwin's guests before a crowded room. She liked nothing more than hearing guests roar with laughter at one of her jokes. Although Mary was quieter, usually preferring to steal away with a book, she and Claire formed a life-long bond, although each sometimes regarded the other as a curse. They frequently played together, sometimes conspiring some new trick to be pulled on the adults.

Mary's half-sister Fanny, the daughter of Gilbert Imlay and Mary Wollstonecraft, was a pale, quiet, obedient girl. She enjoyed little of Mary or her mother's intellectual brilliance or Claire's sparkling personality. Her feelings of inferiority only increased when Godwin published his memoirs of Mary Wollstonecraft, where he wrote openly of the affair with Gilbert Imlay. Fanny could never escape the feeling that something was different about her relationship with her family.

Admiring visitors unwittingly underscored Fanny's feelings of inferiority—and Claire's envy—by constantly remarking of how Mary reminded them of her mother. Often they would ask her to stand beneath her mother's portrait and then exclaim over the resemblance. They never let young Mary forget that the world expected the daughter of Godwin and Wollstonecraft to achieve greatness. One admirer wrote that Mary was "the only offspring of a union that will certainly be matchless in the present generation. ... If you do not remember every word you heard Godwin utter, woe unto you."

Ironically, Godwin's fame as a writer was fading even as expectations for Mary rose. Always controversial, Godwin infuriated England's conservative establishment. His tribute to Wollstonecraft, *Memoirs of the Author of A Vindication of the Rights of Woman,* only made matters worse by revealing his first wife's premarital affairs. Godwin thought it the duty of a

William Godwin's book *Political Justice* made him famous throughout Great Britian

philosopher to seek and write the truth. But the establishment newspapers showed no mercy. The attacks continued until Godwin's career was destroyed. He continued to publish, despite howls of outrage against his work, but never enjoyed the success he had prior to his first marriage. His fall from literary grace had forced him to open the publishing house for children's books. It was Mrs. Godwin's idea, and they used her name—the Juvenile Library of M.J. Godwin & Co.—to avoid the stigma associated with his.

The harsh criticism of Godwin's work did not diminish the enthusiasm of his admirers, some of whom were famous. Mary read books and saw plays by people who were frequent visitors at Skinner Street. Aaron Burr, a former vice-president of the United States, came bearing gifts for the girls and was entertained by them in the second-floor school room which doubled as their "parlor." The poet Samuel Taylor Coleridge read his poems aloud in the parlor.

Visitors doted over the girls so that Mrs. Godwin decided they were a distraction and decreed the girls must stay in their room while they were entertaining guests. Mary, who from a young age loved books and the company of writers, resented the exclusion. Surely her own mother would not have subjected her to such treatment! At the age of six she conspired with Fanny to thwart Mrs. Godwin.

Quickly, before Coleridge began reading one evening, Mary and Fanny hid behind a couch. But Mrs. Godwin caught them by pulling the couch out and exposing the two huddled girls. "Come out at once!" she demanded. But Coleridge took Mary and Fanny's side, insisting they should be allowed to hear the poem. Charming and persuasive, Coleridge won Mrs. Godwin over. Mary listened in awe as Coleridge read "The Rime of the Ancient Mariner," a tale in verse about a cursed sailor forced to endlessly travel the freezing seas of the Arctic. She would never forget the experience. Frozen unexplored wastelands held a lifelong fascination for her.

Literary celebrities of the time would show their lighter side at Skinner Street. The writer and critic Charles Lamb delighted in practical jokes to amuse the children. One night he blew out the table candle during dinner. In the dark, he took the leg of mutton and placed it in the hand of one of the guests. When someone relit the candle, Lamb feigned shock at the "theft."

While he seldom turned anyone away from his table, Godwin had to struggle to keep food on it. He was always strapped for cash and spent a great deal of time trying to arrange loans and gifts from his wealthy followers.

The family publishing company made a small profit, and while Godwin considered it merely a way to make ends meet while he wrote his more important books and essays, the company published some now famous works. Godwin himself wrote several well-received books. Charles and Mary Lamb wrote *Beauty and the Beast* and *Tales from Shakespeare* for the Juvenile Library, and they published the first English version of *Swiss Family Robinson*.

Although the children took most of their lessons from tutors, Godwin insisted on teaching some subjects himself. Mary first learned about the Greek and Roman gods from the pages of his textbook *Pantheon*. Her favorite story was of Prometheus, the giant who stole fire from the gods to give to mortals.

In many ways Mary had a happy childhood. But there was always the tension with her stepmother. Mrs. Godwin had little patience with Mary's reading and imagining, viewing it as a way to avoid doing her chores.

Mary fumed over her stepmother's rebukes. How could she possibly take such an attitude? Mary Wollstonecraft certainly would never have begrudged her time to enrich her mind. Mrs. Godwin's dull ways astonished and depressed her. After all, Papa and her mother had changed the world with their books!

Fighting for her mother's ideals was often painful. Mrs. Godwin would send her proud stepdaughter to pluck her own switches. Mary, always stubborn, refused to cry as the blows rained down. Only her father could bring tears to her eyes by refusing to talk to her.

The tension began to take its toll. One day, when Mary was fourteen, she woke to find her arm prickling with a strange sensation. Soon it was covered with painful bumps. A doctor lanced the bumps and prescribed salt water treatments, only to see them return again.

One of Godwin's admirers came to her rescue. A wealthy Scot sail manufacturer named William Thomas Baxter visited Godwin and noticed Mary's discomfort. Baxter, a generous and open-hearted man, decided that the atmosphere of London was suffocating her spirit. He offered to take Mary to his beautiful seaside home in Dundee. She would be a wonderful companion for Baxter's own daughters. Godwin agreed. He wrote of

Mary's virtues, in contrast to Fanny's, in a letter of advice to Baxter after they had arranged the trip. "My own daughter is considerably superior in capacity to the one her mother had before," Godwin wrote. "Fanny, the eldest, is of a quiet, modest, unshowy disposition. .... Mary, my daughter, is the reverse of her in many particulars. She is singularly bold, somewhat imperious, and active of mind. Her desire of knowledge is great, and her perseverance in everything she undertakes almost invincible. My own daughter is, I believe, very pretty."

In June of 1812, Mary boarded the ship *Osnaburgh* to take her to the Baxter house in Scotland. She boarded alone, a sling around her arm, wondering if she would face a bout of seasickness. The *Osnaburgh* sailed north for a week to the Firth of Tay. At mouth of Dundee Harbor, the captain pointed to the high northern bank to the home of the Baxters. The house was formerly part of on the estate of the Countess of Strathmere. A castle overlooked the Baxter home.

Mary fell in love with the house and grounds, the forest and the beaches. Her bedroom window opened on the spectacular snow-covered Grampian mountains. Mary also grew to love the Baxters. While her father was often taciturn, his emotions bottled tightly inside, Thomas Baxter was congenial and extroverted. His daughter Isobel, studious but affectionate, idolized Mary Wollstonecraft. To a lesser degree, Mary also befriended Baxter's older daughter Christy.

When she first went on hikes with the family, Mary would take a book. But the Baxters soon taught her the joy of physical activity. She became an outdoorswoman, although she still spun her fantasies as she hiked. Mary had always daydreamed, but her gift for weaving fantasy flourished here on the splendid estate. She swam in the bay, raced over the grassy hills, and watched the sunset as she stretched out beneath the canopy of a towering pine grove.

Although Mary kept the somewhat reserved nature she had inherited from her father, she developed the habit of reading the works of her mother aloud to the Baxters after dinner. The family was too traditional to accept all of Wollstonecraft's ideas but were too kind to say so. Mary was sure she was gathering new disciples for her mother's philosophy.

Mary returned home in better health and more beautiful than ever. Although slightly shorter than average, she was delicate-boned and graceful with fair, now unblemished skin. Her luminous hazel eyes, with a streak in the left one that sparkled green, were striking, and her blond hair shone with "sunny and burnished brightness," Claire later wrote.

There were two new disciples frequenting Godwin's parlor when Mary returned. The twenty-year-old nobleman and poet Percy Bysshe Shelley and his teen-age wife Harriet gathered almost daily to hear their mentor Godwin speak on the important issues of the day. Many people thought the handsome Shelley quite mad. At first, Mary thought they were right. But soon she would change her mind.

Mad Shelley

Percy Bysshe Shelley—the middle name rhymes with "wish"—was only the latest of Godwin's young admirers. After reading *Political Justice* he had written to the author that "the name Godwin has been used to excite in me feelings of reverence and admiration." He asked for an opportunity to visit the great man.

Shelley had enthusiastically read *Political Justice*, with its attacks on tradition, organized religion, and the privileges of the wealthy. Godwin's words had confirmed many of the ideas the young poet had come to believe on his own during his unhappy years as a son of a landed, conservative aristocrat, and as a student in England's finest schools.

Shelley's father, Sir Timothy Shelley, had worked hard to impress his oldest son with the values of the wealthy nobility. But Percy, much like Mary, had spent most of his early years on his family estate Field Place reading stories of monsters, witches, and alchemy, and scribbling his own fantasies to be read aloud to his four sisters.

Sent away to school at ten, the unathletic and sensitive Percy soon became the target of bullies. The persecution continued throughout his years at Eton, the school he attended before entering Oxford. The bullying, which many boys endured and eventually learned to accept as part of the tradition of boarding school education, convinced Percy that the entire tradition-bound society—especially his own aristocratic class—was rotten and should be destroyed. Instead of growing into the respectable Sir Percy Shelley as his father had planned, Percy became an enemy of everything his father stood for.

The tension between Shelley and Sir Timothy erupted into the open during his college years, when the young poet collaborated with his Oxford friend Thomas Jefferson Hogg on a pamphlet titled *The Necessity of Atheism*. Shortly after the scandalous tract was published the young men were expelled from Oxford.

After leaving the university, Shelley searched out other radicals ready to war against tradition. Among these was Leigh Hunt, the editor of *The Examiner*, a radical newspaper. Hunt would champion Shelley's poetry for the rest of his life.

To further infuriate his father, Shelly also eloped, in 1811, when he was nineteen, with Harriet Westbrook, the sixteen year old daughter of a retired merchant. Harriet was so beautiful that Coleridge remarked that men tended to forget what they were about to say after glancing her way, but she shared little of Shelley's radical beliefs and secretly hoped to someday settle down to a quiet life as the wife of Sir Percy. Soon she was pregnant and gave birth to a daughter, Ianthe. By the time the couple appeared at Godwin's, Harriet was pregnant again.

Percy Bysshe Shelley wanted to change the world with his poetry

Shelley also began writing poetry. His first major poem, *Queen Mab*, tells the story of a young girl, Ianthe, who meets a fairy named Queen Mab. The fairy takes Ianthe to her palace in space where she sees scenes of the past, present and future. While the scenes of the past and present confirm all of Shelley's disgust with greed and poverty and a world controlled by tyrants, the future is full of the idealistic poet's highest hopes.

Queen Mab was heavily influenced by *Political Justice*. It was shortly after finishing the poem that Shelley had written to Godwin requesting permission to visit at Skinner Street.

Although Godwin no doubt enjoyed the admiration of the talented young poet, he also had a less noble reason for allowing Shelley to become part of his circle. He needed money, and who better to provide it than the wealthy young aristocrat who professed belief in his principles? Soon after his first visit, Shelley began making loans to the older man. Percy, whose angry father had cut off his allowance, was only able to provide the cash by borrowing against his inheritance. Over the next years Godwin's requests for money grew, and there is no record he ever attempted to repay any of the money.

The loans seemed a small price to Percy for his entry into a circle of some of the most celebrated writers and artists in England. Godwin's friends gave Percy's radical ideas far more respect than had his professors at Oxford. Harriet, on the other hand, was more admired for her beauty than her mind. She would sit quietly, looking into the fire, as Shelley, Godwin and other writers debated politics and ethics.

When Mary returned home from Scotland in June of 1814, the ruin of Percy and Harriet's marriage was almost foreordained. Percy not only idolized Godwin, but Mary Wollstonecraft as well. The mere union of their two names in Mary's held a magic for him. Most importantly, unlike Harriet, Mary engaged in conversations about ideas.

Percy's friend Jeff Hogg later wrote of the first time he saw Mary and Shelly together, as he and Percy waited for Godwin in his study. "A thrilling voice called 'Shelley!'," Hogg wrote. "A thrilling voice answered 'Mary'. And he darted out of the room, like an arrow from the bow of the far-shooting king. A very young female, fair and fair-haired, pale indeed, and with a piercing look, wearing a frock of tartan, an unusual dress in London at that time, had called him out of the room."

When Percy returned, Hogg said, "Who was that, pray? A daughter?"

"The daughter of Godwin and Mary," Percy replied. His friend knew well the power of names and words with Percy, and likely suspected the attraction Mary Wollstonecraft Godwin had for him.

Mary at first thought Percy's manner and appearance odd. But as he began following her to her mother's grave at St. Pancras, talking passionately of his ideas and reading his poetry aloud to her, Percy gradually began to win her over. She came to see him as a tragic figure, prevented from reaching his full brilliance as a poet by his family and his marriage to a woman not his equal. While he at first looked gawky to her, Percy now seemed like an angel from one of his own poems, with an unearthly masculine beauty almost too fragile for the common-place world.

The two began to flirt with one another, each wondering if the affection was shared. Percy dropped hints of his growing infatuation, and Mary responded in kind. By the time *Queen Mab* was published, its affectionate dedication to Harriet was outdated. Mary had replaced Harriet in Percy's heart. He wrote an inscription to her on the page containing the dedication. She wrote a inscription of her own. "I have pledged myself to thee, and sacred is the gift," she wrote. "Yes, you are ever with me, sacred vision."

The tension rose as Harriet began to suspect the two. Mary wanted to seal their love affair. On the evening of June 26, 1816, she asked Shelley to join her by the grave of her mother.

The moon rose early, coming up over St. Pancras while the sunset lingered in the west. Shelley opened his heart to Mary, describing his hopes and disappointments. His family and teachers had scorned high ideals, schoolmates had bullied him, he suspected Harriet had been unfaithful. His soft, high voice quavered in urgency and his large eyes bored into Mary's as he told his tale of misery. How could she not believe that every word he said was true?

Shelley pleaded for an angel to save his tortured soul. Could he dare to believe that Mary would deliver him? She trembled. Mary pitied, comforted, and at last, kissed him.

They planned to simply tell Godwin and Harriet that they were in love. Mary wanted Godwin to allow her to join Shelley in a spiritual union without the formality of marriage. Was that not what her father had preached?

Mary soon found out how much different a man her father

Delicate-boned and graceful, young Mary Godwin loved to discuss art and ideas

had become since writing *Political Justice*. Godwin summoned her to his study. He chose not to scold Mary, but to reason with her as an equal. Had she thought about the shame her illicit union with Percy would bring on a family already reviled by the London press for its sins against tradition? And what of her mother's already battered name? The scandal would put yet another blot on Mary Wollstonecraft's reputation.

Mary gave in. She promised she would not see Shelley again, although she could never love another. Satisfied, Godwin had her write a letter to Shelley telling him of her decision.

After reading the note, Shelley made a public spectacle of his sorrow. Mary heard rumors that he had threatened suicide. Early one morning, Percy came to Skinner Street with the apparent intention of making good on the threat. He burst through the door shortly after Godwin left, eyes red and clothes disheveled, and thrust into Mary's hand a bottle of laudanum, a narcotic which could kill in overdose.

"They wish to separate us, my beloved, but we shall be united in death," Shelley cried. "Drink this and you shall escape their tyranny!"

He yanked a pistol from his pocket and brandished it. "This shall enable me to join you, and we shall be reunited for all time!" he shouted to Mary.

Mrs. Godwin, unshaken by Shelley's theatrical scene, joined with a family friend to grab the gun from his hand. Mary dutifully poured out the laudanum, keeping her thoughts to herself. The power of Percy's love seemed nearly invincible! Little by little, Percy was breaking down Mary's determination to keep her promise to her father.

The lovers arranged a rendezvous on the afternoon of July 26, 1814. Mary and Claire pretended to want to go for a walk. But they walked only far enough to meet Percy in a park. Although Claire was dying to hear what was said, the couple made her wait out of earshot. Later they told her their plans, which included Claire.

They planned to elope in a coach after midnight, and race down the cobblestone roads to the coast and to France. Claire was to join them as an interpreter. Neither Mary nor Percy spoke French. The young idealists were about to put the early philosophy of William Godwin to the test, to the horror of the Godwin and Shelley families, and the delight of all in Europe who loved gossip and scandals.

Romance

Percy Shelley spent the evening of July 27, 1814 in a fever of anticipation. Would he finally make his longed-for break for freedom, with Mary at his side? Or would the Godwins again dash their plans? He had arranged for a coach to meet them before sunup. The hours dragged at an agonizing pace to the appointed hour of 4 a.m.

The lovers met at the entrance of Hatton Garden. Claire and Mary arrived about fifteen minutes late, for Claire had to return after breaking the heel of her shoe while sneaking out of the house. Then, adding to Shelley's frenzy, Mary remembered she had neglected to write her father a note. Claire and Shelly waited while Mary raced back to Skinner Street and penned her farewell message to Godwin.

"How dreadful did this time appear," Percy later wrote. "It seemed we trifled with life and hope."

But after a few minutes, Mary hurried back to Hatton Garden. The three young people scrambled into the coach, and it sped away toward Dover, with Mary in Percy's arms. The day turned suffocatingly hot after sunrise, and Mary came close to fainting several times. When they reached Dover, she cooled herself with a brief dip in the ocean. Percy and Claire took care of the business of securing passage across the English Channel. Some sailors refused to sail because they feared a storm that evening. But Claire and Percy found a boat and by six in the evening persuaded a crew to carry them.

Just after nightfall a swift, violent storm struck, rocking the skiff's mast as the boat heeled and skipped water. A fierce northeaster pushed them toward Calais. Mary spent a restless night, asking over and over if they were nearing the French shore. A sudden thud sounded against the hull, and Mary woke to find the morning sun in her eyes.

"Mary, look," Percy said, as though seeing a new world, "the sun rises over France."

They were to suffer miserable conditions in France. But throughout it all, all three felt they had embarked on a grand adventure. A young, impractical nobleman and two well-schooled daughters of a literary family, they nonetheless considered themselves social rebels. Mary, at sixteen, had never wavered in believing it to be her destiny to achieve great things. Percy carried egotism a step further, imagining himself in his wildest flights as a poetic angel sent to improve humankind. "It was acting a novel, being an incarnate romance," Mary later wrote.

The adventure thrilled Claire as well. One Swiss gentleman asked if she, too, had run away for love. "Oh, dear, no!" Claire laughed. "I came to speak French."

But Claire could be practical as well as mischievous. She

discovered a cheap and clean lodging house. The trio had not planned to stay long in Calais, but they met with an unpleasant surprise before traveling further. The captain of the ship showed up at their lodgings to announce that "a fat lady" had arrived, inquiring after them. Mrs. Godwin had tracked them down.

Mary refused to see her and went upstairs. Percy did not bother to speak to her either. But Claire did meet with Mrs. Godwin, who used every argument to attempt to persuade her to give up her adventure, to return with her to England and end this family disgrace. Long into the night they argued. Claire asked her to stay the night, and Mrs. Godwin accepted. Yet neither got much sleep. Before breakfast, Claire told her mother she would stay with Mary and Percy.

Mary took the news as a victory, all the sweeter as a triumph over her detested stepmother. She hardly seemed to notice that she and her lover had acquired Claire in the bargain. Many times in the future, Mary would wonder if her victory over Mrs. Godwin had been worth the price.

They arrived in Paris, dazzled and penniless. The city was famed for the splendor it offered young lovers, but the trio could enjoy few of its pleasures until Shelley pawned some of his possessions, including his watch and chain. He also borrowed some money from a French businessman who knew his family. The three used the money to buy bread and wine, and to dine at the outdoor cafes. Looking out over the Seine river, they discussed the works they were writing, such as Mary's strangely-titled *Hate*, a novel that was never published. They also talked of the works of Wollstonecraft and Godwin, whose radical ideas had propelled these young people toward their own rebellion.

When they decided it was time to continue their travels, Percy sent Claire and Mary to an ass merchant with the money to buy an animal. They returned with a donkey. With Mary astride the donkey, the three set off to Switzerland. With Mary and Claire clad in black silk dresses, they looked a strange mix of poverty and privilege.

Before long, a new problem vexed them. The old donkey's strength gave out, and they had to sell him for a mule. Then Percy twisted his ankle. Mary let Percy ride the mule, while she and Claire trudged behind. When night fell, they had to depend on the generosity of peasants for lodging. They slept in the dirtiest beds Mary had ever seen. "Let me observe here that the inhabitants were not in the habit of washing themselves either when they rose or went to bed," Mary wrote in the journal she shared with Percy. Claire complained that rats scrabbled over her face with their cold paws.

The trip held delights Mary would never forget. She loved living free of the disciplined routine at Skinner Street. She and Percy could decide on a whim to take a picnic under a tree by the shore, with no one to tell them when their meal or talk must end. Reading aloud to one another was more pleasant than reading alone, they discovered, and their bond grew stronger as they shared their secrets.

Less pleasant was growth of the rivalry between Claire and Mary. Claire was an incurable flirt, and it soon became hard to tell when she crossed the line from flirtation. Mary's dilemma was complicated by her belief in free love and disdain for jealousy. Claire enjoyed the game of seeing how far she could push her step-sister with her behavior toward Shelley.

Like Percy, Claire loved to tell and listen to ghost stories. She let the tales drive her into a state of near-panic just before bedtime. Then, after everyone had settled in for the night, Claire would run shrieking into Mary and Percy's bedroom. Spectres, ghosts, phantasms, Claire said, had pursued her into her bed. The only cure—certainly the only way to get her to settle down—was for Claire to climb into bed with Mary and Percy. So Mary could almost never rid herself of Claire, day or night.

Their trip ended abruptly. In the village of Brunnen, they found themselves dazzled by the natural beauty. Despite their shortage of funds Percy leased a house for six months. That night, Mary and Percy had a talk. They had outrun the purse strings of their families, and bartered away everything of worth they had brought with them. The conclusion was unavoidable. "Determined at last to return to England," Mary wrote in their journal.

They decided on an inexpensive but scenic route home— down the Rhine River by boat, then to Germany and Holland. Mary later borrowed some of the scenery of *Frankenstein* from the majestic sights. Steep rocks and mountains overhung the water, and beautiful castles overlooked many cliffs, while battered fortresses with crumbling towers nestled in the crevasses. The scenery awed Mary, but some of the other passengers disgusted her. She described some of the foreigners, with their coarse habits and food, as "slimy." "T'were easier for god to make entirely new men than to attempt to purify such monsters as these," she wrote in the journal.

The river became treacherous; their craft battled dangerous currents and eddies, stopping for short periods at various villages. Two days after Mary's seventeenth birthday, their boat tied at Gernsheim, under the ruined castle of a noble family— the Frankensteins. The local people told many stories about the family, including a legend that one of the barons had slain a dragon.

Return To Reality

The three travelers arrived back in England to encounter a cold reception. It seemed that all of London chattered about the wicked couple who had deserted their famous families, as well as the young nobleman's wife and two children. Rumors spread about what the three had done during their jaunt across northern Europe. Some slanderers even dared to say that Godwin had "sold" Mary and Claire to the well-heeled young Percy. Godwin was used to being defamed in the press. But this latest round of indignities lashed him into a rare fury.

Godwin punished Mary in his cruelest manner, by refusing to talk with her. The couple's only news from the Godwins came from Mary's step-brother Charles, who took it on himself to act as the messenger from Skinner Street. Godwin had turned his back on Percy as well, except through the messages sent to extract money. The Godwins' sympathies all lay with Harriet, Percy's spurned wife. As for the money, Percy and Godwin still agreed on one point: Shelley's wealthy family had no natural right to the money, and the young poet still owed his monetary support to the older man of letters.

Godwin was not the only one hounding Percy for money, adding to the infamy he and Mary inherited on returning to their native land. Their first afternoon back in London, the couple rode to Shelley's bank to withdraw the funds to set up house-keeping. They were stunned when the banker informed them that Harriet had withdrawn every pound in the account.

To make matters worse, Harriet's creditors joined the pack. They badgered and so persistently dunned Percy that he, Mary and Claire were forced from their modest quarters to an even cheaper hotel. Mary suffered a shock that fall, when she found out she was pregnant, with the baby to be born near the time of Harriet's next child.

The three would sometimes find their escape in reading, meeting friends of Mary's father and, especially delightful to Percy and Claire, discovering the occasional addition to their collection of occult tales. Once their weird conversation wandered over such strange speculations that none of them could sleep until dawn. Claire would often babble nonsensically after such sessions.

One night, Clair insisted strange creatures had approached her in the dark. The furniture had walked on its own. After the sun rose, Mary wrote a joking description in her journal: "The next morning the chimney board in Jane's (Claire's) room is found to have walked leisurely into the middle of the room, accompanied by the pillow, who, being very sleepy, tried to get into bed again, but sat down on his back."

The relentless creditors were not so easily laughed away. Once Percy had to spend a night in jail because Mary could not immediately raise the money for his bail. After the authorities let him go, the couple arranged rendezvous points where they could meet without running into the constables. Mary and Percy would steal away to cafes, coffeehouses, public parks, churches, and of course, Mary Wollstonecraft's grave.

In November, Harriet gave birth to a son named Charles. The letter notifying Percy was signed "Your deserted wife." Despite his and Harriet's estrangement, Percy sent joyful notes to his relatives and friends. Yet Mary did not share his happiness. Her nerves nearly buckled under the strain of her illegitimate and very public relationship with Percy. "Every church in England should ring at the birth of the Harriet's and Percy's baby," she wrote in her journal. "It is the son of his *wife*."

Mary began to realize what a harsh world the child of her relationship with Percy would face. Godwin's philosophy had described a world where no woman or man would have to bow unwillingly to the institution of marriage. But while Harriet's child was born to inherit the name and wealth of the Shelleys, people would call the child of Percy and Mary a "bastard." She slowly began to realize that the rules of Godwinism, a philosophy she had accepted without question since childhood, wielded little power with most of society.

Then fate dealt Mary a crippling, blow. Her baby, a daughter, was born prematurely on February 22, 1815. Two weeks later, the infant died.

What had she done to deserve such pain, Mary wondered? It was as though she were cursed! The shock almost literally knocked the breath from her. She did not speak for two days.

Percy took care of her until he was exhausted, with some help from his old school mate, Thomas Jefferson Hogg. Hogg had courted Mary for a while himself, before she fell so deeply in love with Shelley. And he was still attracted to her. But he acted only as her friend now, nursing Mary, preparing meals, keeping house.

Godwin had taught Mary that mature people did not "indulge" themselves in grief and mourning. But how could Mary refrain from grieving? " ... think of my little dead baby," she wrote in her journal on March 13, "this is foolish I suppose yet whenever I am left alone to my own thoughts & do not read to divert them they always come back to the same point—that I was a mother & am so no longer."

Six days later, she had a strange dream. "Dream that my little baby came to life again—that it had only been cold & that we rubbed it by the fire & it lived—I awake & find no baby—I think about the little thing all day ..."

Ironically, another death provided some material comfort to the young outcasts. Shelley's grandfather died, leaving a quarter-million pounds for his heir. The will worked to the advantage of both Percy and his father Sir Timothy. Percy could claim a portion of his inheritance immediately. Sir Timothy was happy to pay off the most publicly-ridiculed scandal-monger of his family, settle Percy's most ruinous debts, and establish a trust fund of one thousand pounds per year for life. Thus Sir Timothy would rid himself of at least some of the shame heaped on his name. And, of course, Percy did not quibble for a moment with the terms.

Percy's inheritance brought an end, for the time, to dodging constables and debt collectors and to living in squalid rooms. Claire, who had become an intrusive nuisance to Mary, won some money in a lottery and decided to go off on a long holiday. As the leaves and flowers sprouted in the spring of 1815, the burst of financial good luck revived Mary's spirits. How wonderful it felt, just to go to a cafe without looking over their shoulders for the constables!

They moved to Bathgate outside London. In July, Mary's delight increased when she found she was pregnant again.

The move brought a dramatic improvement in their lives and health. After the death of her baby, Mary had become extraordinarily pale and thin. Percy wrote that she had regained her beauty. Shelley's writing had suffered as he had dodged creditors in the city, but now he threw his energy into his creative labors.

They gloried in each other's revival. Percy and Mary now developed habits which they would follow in the best of times for the rest of their lives together. He would awake at about eight, an hour before Mary rose. After a light breakfast, they would separate and follow their separate pursuits until lunch. Then they would go to their respective desks. Percy devoted himself solely to writing, while Mary mixed writing and reading. Although her father was not yet speaking to her, Mary dutifully followed in the scholarly manner in which she was brought up. The two would reunite for a late lunch, typically a soup, roast, vegetables, and fruit and cheese for dessert. For two hours in the evening they left literature and writing behind for a walk in the woods. They changed into the stout footwear which served as "walking shoes" for the time, but Percy dressed otherwise in the style of noble townsman, while Mary wore ankle-length skirts and petticoats.

Although they had already written of their love as though it personified a heavenly ideal, their bond grew stronger as it matured. Mary learned to love the child in Percy. She discovered he was incapable of being near a lake shore for long without ripping a sheet from his notebook and fashioning a toy boat from it.

Mary's second baby was born on January 24, 1816. The labor went well and the couple named the boy William, after Mary's father. But William Godwin, who had written years ago that children born outside wedlock should bear no stigma, did not acknowledge the child's birth nor break his vow of silence toward Mary. At the same time, he continued his demands for money from Percy.

Percy raised the money, but he also contemplated some choice words for Godwin. He still respected Godwin as a writer and philosopher, but the snub toward his son drove Percy to rake Godwin in his next letter with terms harsher than Godwin had ever read from his young disciple: "In my judgment, neither I nor your daughter, nor her offspring, ought to encounter the treatment which we receive on every side," Percy wrote. "Do not talk of forgiveness again to me, for my blood boils in my veins, and my gall rises against all that bears the human form, when I think of what I, their benefactor and ardent lover, have endured of enmity and contempt."

Godwin made no reply. But the young couple had learned to live comfortably with neither their parents' nor society's approval. They were happy in their little cottage near Bishopsgate, the place they lived the longest of any during their union. Ignoring the snubs of the world, they were beginning to find peace within themselves. It lasted until May of 1816, when Claire arrived with a bewitching and intriguing scheme.

During her time away from them, Claire had found adventure on her own. She, too, wanted romance and chose as the object of her affections one of the most sought-after men in London. His name was George Gordon, or Lord Byron, the sixth Baron of his line. He was a poet best-known for his work *Childe Harold's Pilgrimage*. London society thought him one of its most dashing bachelors and almost certainly the city's most wicked.

Byron was tall and handsome, with long dark hair and the chiseled features of a stage actor. At 28, he was so beguiling that, the gossips said, no woman could resist him. That may have been an exaggeration, but many titled women had indeed given in to temptation, and he was notorious for his affairs. Like a modern rock star, Byron was followed by hordes of admirers. He received love letters from women who had never met him.

The famed poet was "mad, bad and dangerous to know," in the words of one of his former lovers. In truth, Lord Byron had learned to mask his insecurities behind an image of spectacular decadence and perversion. He was club-footed, and though this single physical flaw sometimes tormented him, he rarely spoke of it. It certainly made little difference to his lovers, among them

Lord Byron was the most notorious poet in London

his half-sister Augusta. He kept locks of his lovers' hair in marked envelopes as trophies of his "conquests." When one of the women he had cast aside asked him for a lock of his own hair, Byron cruelly sent her instead a curl from his current mistress. When asked what kind of woman he liked, he said he was an admirer of the "harem principle," in which one man enjoys the physical charms of many women.

Many people were offended by Byron's behavior, but few denied his literary talents When the first two parts of *Childe Harold's Pilgrimage* appeared in 1812, the first edition sold out in three days and the poet became the talk of London.

Byron had recently separated from his wife, a fact which doubtless fueled Claire's ambition. She sent him one of the love letters he had come to consider commonplace. Byron did not respond. Only when she wrote him that she was Godwin's stepdaughter did he reply. He admired Godwin, and having heard of his financial troubles, had considered lending him some money.

Byron was a director at a theater on Drury Lane. One day Claire showed up, supposedly for an audition as a singer. She flirted outrageously with Byron, enough to disarm even a man accustomed to the attention of women. At first, he did not return her advances. But Claire threw herself at him so persistently, she finally triumphed, and the two became lovers. Yet the fickle Byron much preferred brief affairs to commitments. Perhaps to break their bond, Byron began planning to leave England.

Claire was determined not to be cast aside so easily. She came to Bathgate with an intriguing proposal. She told Mary and

Percy of her relationship with Byron, leaving out the fact of her affair. How would they like to meet the great poet?

Claire's news astonished and thrilled Mary. She had grown up around writers, but Byron was currently the sensation of London. She was almost star-struck the afternoon she and Claire met Byron at his Piccadilly mansion. She had expected to discover him a roguish devil, but Byron put on his most charming manners.

"How mild he is! How gentle! How different from what I expected," Mary said to Claire.

Mary had read Byron's poetry aloud to Percy during their courtship and first travels abroad. Great things could come of a meeting between such brilliant poets as Shelley and Byron. And Claire could easily arrange for the three to meet Byron at Lake Geneva in Switzerland. Beguiled by the clever Claire, the two decided to take her up on her offer. They packed their trunks, along with little William, and sailed for Geneva the first week of May.

The Monster's Tale

More patient travelers might have waited out the spring storms that lashed the roads leading to the summit of the Jura mountains during that May of 1816. But Mary and Percy would not be restrained. The two, along with Claire, retraced much of the route they had traveled two years before. The violent weather seemed like a romantic backdrop for the beginning of their adventure. They paid little attention to the dangers of riding over twisting, desolate mountain roads in pelting rain and snow.

Three days after leaving Paris they arrived at the town of Poligny at the foot of the Jura. They spent much of the day finding horses, then rashly traveled on as evening fell, struggling up the mountain by moonlight. Four horses pulled the carriage as ten men steadied it. On one side of the steep road the peaks of mountains loomed, barely visible through the mist and downpour. The other side was a sheer drop, filled with swirling clouds. They arrived at the town of Champagnolles by midnight, charged with the energy of their adventure, and started again early the next morning, climbing through mountain ravines and valleys.

"Sometimes the road winds high into the regions of the frost, and then the forests become scattered, and the branches of the trees are loaded with snow, and half of the enormous pines themselves buried in the wavy drifts," Mary wrote. "The spring, as the inhabitants informed us, was unusually late and indeed the cold was excessive ..." Shafts of sunlight broke through the snow clouds in the afternoon, setting the snowflakes aglow like bright sparks.

In fact, Mary's party had seen but a preview of the strange weather that would inspire her and her friends to tell each other ghost stories until late at night. That year Europe recorded its coldest temperatures ever. In America, people called 1816 the "Year Without a Summer." Astrologers peering into their telescopes discovered spots on the sun. Some preachers told their flocks that the end of time was at hand. Such dire prophesies did nothing to dampen the enthusiasm of the literary pilgrims, who thrilled at the spectacles staged by nature throughout their months at Lake Geneva.

Mary, Percy and Claire met Lord Byron at a hotel beneath the Alps. Byron arrived with his traveling doctor and friend, John Polidori, a handsome young man. The meeting went awkwardly, partly because Byron was not delighted about a reunion with Claire. Shelley and Byron, however, soon discovered they had much in common, and within a week the Byron and Shelley parties rented neighboring cottages on the shores of Lake Geneva.

Mary and Percy moved into *Maison Chapius*. Byron moved further up the slope, in the more magnificent *Villa Diodati*, with its iron balcony overlooking the lake, and bordered on one side by a hillside vineyard. Mary and Percy could hike through the vineyard to Byron's villa in about ten minutes. Claire and Byron soon resumed their affair.

Byron established himself as the informal leader of the group. He was the most famous, while Percy's works had been read by few. Mary was uncomfortably reminded that she had not yet fulfilled the destiny so many expected for her. As for Polidori, he was a literary enthusiast but not a serious writer.

When the group socialized it was on Byron's schedule, which meant late nights. Yet Mary and Percy kept the same work habits they had established at their English house at Bathgate, with each rising promptly and early for morning writing and study.

The widely-known—some said infamous—English travelers on Lake Geneva created a sensation some tourists found more interesting than the scenery. Wild rumors spread. People wondered what the notoriously free-spirited daughter of Godwin and Wollstonecraft, the atheist Shelley, and the infernally wicked Byron were doing behind the walls of their villas. People rented telescopes to spy on them. It is no wonder that when the curiosity-seekers found little to satisfy their desire for scandal they invented details. But Mary knew little of the lurid stories. All she knew was that in the clean air of the sparkling Alps she was beginning to feel more alive than ever before.

"I feel happy as a new-fledged bird," she wrote her sister Fanny, "and hardly care what twig I fly to, so that I may try my new-found wings." Percy bought a sailboat and the entire party spent every evening boating on the lake, except for those when

Claire Clairmont was Lord Byron's lover during the summer of 1816

high winds or thunderstorms threatened.

Indeed, the spirit of renewal Mary wrote of seemed to touch everyone. Percy and Byron talked into the night, about philosophy, science and religion. Mary was well-schooled in these subjects, having grown up in the company of famed scholars and writers, but she listened more than she talked. Claire joined in when the talk turned to tales and speculation on the supernatural.

Claire and Percy resumed their antics. Percy would run through the house shrieking at the top of his lungs, jabbering about some ghostly vision he had seen. Always eager to join Percy in any game that excluded Mary, Claire also screeched at imagined specters and egged Percy on. On one occasion, Percy's ranting went on so long that Byron and Polidori chased him down, tied him with rope and gagged him. Mary spent an hour soothing him, then untied him.

As always, Mary kept a tighter rein on her emotions than Percy did. But she loved the ghostly tales. They all delighted in the eerie folklore of the area. With the deep, resonant voice so suited to his poetry, Byron would read aloud from *Fantasmagoriana*, a book of supernatural stories he had bought from a Genevan bookseller.

The book was a treasure chest of horrors. In "La Morte Fiancee," a man abandons his wife-to-be for another and is chased down and killed by his fiance's relentless ghost. One of the stories told several tales in one, as a group of travelers talked of their individual encounters with ghostly beings. In another tale, a man kissed his wife on his wedding night to discover that she had become the corpse of a previous lover.

It would have been impossible for a group of writers to discover such pleasure in folk stories without trying to write their own. Byron closed the book one night and offered a challenge to the group. "We will each write a ghost story," he said, as Mary and Percy prepared to leave. To Mary he said "You and I will publish ours together."

The challenge thrilled Mary. For several years she had been seeking a project which would prove her worthy of her parents' legacy. Perhaps this ghost story would be a good start.

Yet writing such a story was not as easy as the stories in *Fantasmagoriana* made it appear. For one thing, Mary found that inspiration often vanished with the sunrise, when her carefree existence by the lake banished the fear of ghosts and phantoms. For another, she was intimidated by Percy and Lord Byron. Percy had at least published some of his work, and Lord Byron had built a towering reputation. Mary developed a case of "writer's block"—a miserable state in which a writer is unable to put words on paper.

The others began to prod her. Each morning someone would ask "Have you thought of a story?" No, she was forced to reply. Her failure humiliated her. How could she fail after all her family and society expected of her? How could she come up with nothing, when her companions' work was going so well?

Actually, the others had achieved less than Mary thought. Percy started a story about a ghost made of ashes, but he quickly lost interest. His talent lay in poetry. Dr. Polidori devoted himself to his story about a vampire, and labored over it throughout the summer. His book, *The Vampyre*, would eventually be published and enjoy popular success. But it would not be remembered, because the doctor's writing talent did not equal that of his summer companions. Claire did not write anything. As for Byron, he too began a vampire story, discarded it, then later used parts of "The Vampire" in his poem *Mazeppa*. Percy and Byron preferred talking about supernatural horrors and scientific marvels to writing about them.

One night Byron and Percy talked until after midnight about an experiment by Dr. Erasmus Darwin that challenged traditional ideas about the nature of life itself. Darwin was said to have made a piece of vermicelli, a string of dough thinner than spaghetti, move on its own volition. If such a thing could be, the men wondered, what were the limits of science? Perhaps a corpse would be reanimated someday.

What a horrible thought! The image of the revived corpse stuck in Mary's mind as she prepared for bed. How more gruesome than even the stories in *Fantasmagoriana*. But she was still more worried by another fear—that she would continue to flounder in her quest for a story. Failure could mean she had inherited none of her parents' genius! When Mary lay down that night, she knew sleep would not come easily.

She closed her eyes, but could not sleep as she imagined the thing squirming in Dr. Darwin's glass cage. Science might unleash terrors worse than any the old story tellers had ever dreamed of. People had long-ago formed their ideas of what ghosts and devils looked like, and the curses they could bring. But who knew anything about the possible monsters of science?

Perhaps a corpse could be reanimated?

Eventually, Mary entered a state between sleep and wakefulness. Eerie illustrations of her fears began to flash in her head. A man knelt beside the body he had created with his own hands—a pieced together monster. She could hear the thoughts of the creature's creator as the thing began to move. "I saw the hideous phantasm of a man stretched out, and then, on the working of some powerful engine, show signs of life, and stir with uneasy, half-vital motion," Mary wrote later. At the idea of defying God, fear gripped the maker of the thing.

"Frightful must it be; for supremely frightful would be the effect of any human endeavor to mock the stupendous mechanism of the Creator of the world. His success would terrify the artist; he would rush away from his odious handiwork, horror-stricken. He would hope that, left to itself, the slight spark of life which he had communicated would fade; that this thing which had received such imperfect animation would subside into dead matter; and he might sleep in the belief that the silence of the grave would quench forever the transient existence of the hideous corpse which he had looked upon as the cradle of life."

The man who had raised the dead would seek refuge in his own bed. But sleep would offer no refuge for the monster-maker. "He sleeps; but he is awakened; he opens his eyes; behold the horrid thing stands at his bedside, opening his curtains, and looking on him with yellow, watery, but speculative eyes."

Mary opened her own eyes. Fully awake now, she tried to rid herself of the horrible vision that had come from her subconscious mind. She looked beyond the curtains bordering her bed, at the dark room dimly streaked by moonlight breaking through the shutters. In her mind's eye, she would see the moonlit lake and the encircling Alps beyond the shuttered window. Yet her waking nightmare had shattered the comforts of reality. Mary could only see the monster's watery eyes.

For days she had unsuccessfully searched her mind for some frightful story. But on a night when she had sought only sleep, her awful phantasm had come looking for her. Joy quickly replaced fear. "I have found it!" she wrote, describing her thoughts that night. "What terrified me will terrify others; and I need only describe the specter which had haunted my midnight pillow."

Mary began writing the next day with the words "It was on a dreary night in November," then wrote a short story closely based on her dream. When she showed it to Percy, he was so impressed he urged her to write a longer work. She followed his advice, and set about writing a novel. Although much was to happen before the book was completed—much of it tragic— eleven months later she finished her tale. It was titled after the name she had given the creature's creator, the same as that of the noble family whose castles she had seen along the Rhine river: *Frankenstein*.

Since its publication in 1818, *Frankenstein* has never gone out of print. It inspired a play in her lifetime, and movies, stories and other books long afterward. Most importantly, it did what Mary wanted most for her tale—it made her readers shudder.

What has kept *Frankenstein* alive almost two centuries after it was written? There are many reasons. For one, the tale is not just another ghost story. It is perhaps the first modern myth, posing the age old question: In our search for knowledge about the mysteries of creation, are some questions better left unanswered? The story of Doctor Frankenstein is one of those tales that seems to have always existed, one that wasn't written so much as it was recorded. But that is inaccurate. The story came directly from the mind, experience, and talent of nineteen year old Mary Shelley.

Although Mary still claimed to believe in her father's philosophy when she began *Frankenstein*, much of the book's tension comes from her questioning of some of Godwin's deepest beliefs. She also used the oldest storyteller's tool. She asked the question "What if?" and attempted to answer with a story. What if a human seeking truth discovered too much knowledge? What if the quest for a perfect man led instead to the creation of a monster? It is on this last point that *Frankenstein* contradicts Godwinism, by suggesting that a search for the highest knowledge could unleash monsters.

Frankenstein is structured as a story within a story. One tale is that of the narrator Robert Walton, an explorer sailing toward the North Pole, hoping to achieve fame in the process of discovery. One fog-choked afternoon, Walton and his crew observe a dog sled pulling someone who at a distance appears to be a giant. The sailors watch with their telescopes until the giant disappears. The next day, Walton's crew rescues a lost man floating on a fragment of ice with his sled. Walton eventually befriends the man. He learns that his name is Victor

Frankenstein. With some prodding, Walton persuades Franken-stein to explain how he came to be stranded in the cold Arctic.

Frankenstein is a son of a respected family in Geneva, Switzerland. As a young man he enrolled in the University of Ingolstadt. His professors' lessons in medicine and biology fire Frankenstein's intellectual curiosity, and his faith in his own genius leads him to ponder the seemingly impossible. He embarks on a quest to create life. He uses corpses for his experiments, working in an attic. Frankenstein is sometimes disgusted by the methods he must use, and comes to consider his attic laboratory his "workshop of filthy creation." Yet he forces himself to press on, and one November night, succeeds in bringing to life a creature made from the dead.

The creature's seeping yellow eye opens. The sight of his creation stirring shakes Frankenstein into the realization of what he has done. In his feverish desire to see his intellectual quest succeed, he had imagined the misshapen dead giant at his feet a man of beauty.

But Frankenstein's breath catches in his throat as he surveys the Monster. "Great God!" Frankenstein exclaims to Walton. "His yellow skin scarcely covered the work of muscles and arteries beneath; his hair was of a lustrous black, and flowing; his teeth of pearly whiteness; but these luxuriences only formed a more horrid contrast with his watery eyes, that seemed almost of the same color as the dun white sockets in which they were set, his shriveled complexion and black lips."

The Monster is so frightening Frankenstein flees from it. The creature escapes the laboratory, only to find himself shunned by every terrified human who lays eyes on him. He eventually teaches himself to speak and read by spying on a country family. The monster's attempts to find peace in the world are always shattered by the assaults of humans revolted by his appearance. In turn, the Monster becomes violent. He kills Frankenstein's brother. Frankenstein hunts the creature down, determined to rid the world of it.

But on their meeting, Frankenstein's Monster persuades his creator that he has a right to live. The thing's loneliness and pain touch Frankenstein's heart. The creature promises he will leave the civilized world, if only Frankenstein will grant his single wish—a bride, created in the same manner in which he was made. Frankenstein agrees and travels to the Orkney Islands, off the Northern coast of Scotland, and sets up another laboratory. But the task proves even harder than it was the first time, and Frankenstein is overcome by his loathing. He tears the body of the female creature to pieces without attempting to bring it to life. This enrages the Monster, who has been spying on him all along. The creature leaves his creator with a threat. "It is well," the Monster says. "I go, but remember, I shall be with you on your wedding night."

The creature carries out his vow. He murders Frankenstein's bride Elizabeth as the couple honeymoons on Lake Como. Frankenstein chases his creature throughout Europe and Russia, and finally into the frozen Arctic. The chase wears down Frankenstein's once inexhaustible energy, and he tells Walton his tale as he nears death. After writing down Frankenstein's tale, Walton walks the deck of his ship, listening to the breezes and the waves as he considers the story. From below he hears an odd sound.

It sounds like a voice, but one impossibly hoarse for a human. Walton goes below, into Frankenstein's cabin. Frankenstein is dead. Over him stands a towering creature, with long ragged hair, its huge hands outstretched. The Monster is shaken by grief.

"That also is my victim," the Monster cries. "In his murder, my crimes are consummated!" The Monster then makes a suicide vow, and gives his own eulogy before diving into the icy northern ocean: "I shall ascend my funeral pile triumphantly, and exult in the agony of the torturing flames," the Monster proclaims. "The light of that conflagration will fade away, my ashes will be swept into the sea by the winds. My spirit will sleep in peace; or if it thinks, it will not surely think thus. Farewell!"

But does Frankenstein's Monster really end his own life? Mary's simple description of the Walton's last sight of the monster leaves the question open. "He sprung from the cabin-window, as he said this, upon the ice-raft which lay close to the vessel. He was soon borne away by the waves and lost in darkness and distance."

Tales of vampires and ghosts, such as the ones Mary and her companions read aloud at Lake Geneva, were long-standing traditions of folklore. *Frankenstein* did not follow the old rules of gothic stories. The book bridges the gap between gothic and science fiction, a genre that had not yet been invented. Mary achieved this breakthrough by asking questions others had ignored. Even so, Mary did not create her story from thin air.

She said as much in her introduction to the book: "Invention, it must be humbly admitted, does not exist in creating out of void, but out of chaos; the materials must, in the first place be afforded: it can give form to dark, shapeless substances, but cannot bring into being the substance itself."

While the well-known legend of Faust, the man who trades his soul to Satan for knowledge, provided part of the model for Victor Frankenstein, Mary took a great deal of her material from the exciting changes occurring in science during the late years of the 1700s and the early years of the 1800s. In 1789, an Italian physiologist named Luigi Galvani made a discovery that would make the speculations of Frankenstein seem to be within the bounds of possibility. He found that an electric current passed through the legs of dead frogs caused their limbs to twitch. Galvani was but one of the pioneers of electricity, a new science which would uncover forces never before imagined.

Mary's father, William Godwin, also thought scientific discoveries would help liberate humankind. By questioning the proper limits of science, Mary both rejected her father's faith in progress and aligned herself with the romantic writers, such as the Frenchman Jean Jacques Rosseau, who argued humans were at their best in the "natural" state.

The strange tale also rejected Godwin's faith in reason to answer all problems. Victor Frankenstein, a man of science who, if Godwin was correct, would let reason dictate his decisions, is driven to destruction by an all-consuming passion for knowledge. Mary's seems to be arguing that reason and rationalism only extends so far. We all have the capacity to go "over-the-edge," into dark, internal spaces that are immune to the calming influences of reason.

Mary professed Godwinism throughout her life, perhaps in deference to her famous father. But she was principally a Romantic writer. She demonstrated as much in both in her style of writing and her approach to life. Romantic writers wrote fewer tracts and works of philosophy, concentrating instead on fiction, poetry, and drama, often set in exotic times and places to create an intense atmosphere, as Mary did in Frankenstein's chase through the dark forests of Russia and the North Pole.

When Byron threw out his literary dare—"We will each write a ghost story"—he probably had in mind a more or less traditional Gothic story. But Mary was not so easily satisfied. She had been raised to meet high standards in her life and work. That is perhaps one reason why she had to endure the agony of the creative drought before she came up with an idea.

If Mary had been content with less, she might have turned out a ghost or vampire story of the typical sort, as did her summer companion Dr. John Polidori with his lightly regarded *The Vampyre*. By forcing her subconscious mind to plumb its depths for a tale she considered worthy of her pen, she created a vision beyond anything imagined by the Gothic writers. The result was a work of authentic genius which has continued to dazzle, intrigue and horrify readers to the present day.

Suicides

The pace of Mary's now turbulent life increased during the eleven months it took to write *Frankenstein*. She spent August 9, 1816 writing, pleased with the progress she was making, when her work was interrupted by a disturbing letter from Fanny. Mary and Percy often ignored the sufferings of others in their happiness, Fanny's letter began. As usual, Mary's self-sacrificing half-sister did not dwell on her own problems, but on those of Godwin, who was fighting a daily battle with his creditors. The love-struck couple knew little of poor William Godwin's troubles, Fanny charged, because "you often deceive yourself about things." Fanny pounded the desperate message home with her closing words: "Write small, for Mamma complains of the double postage of a double letter. I pay the full postage of all the letters I send, and you know I have not a sou of my own. ... I am not well; my mind always keeps my body in a fever; but never mind me. Adieu, my dear sister. Let me entreat you to consider seriously all I have said concerning your father."

Fanny had known for a long time that she was not Godwin's

child. The knowledge only made her more devoted to Godwin and her step-mother, and grateful for any affection shown her. She rarely complained, and suffered her frequent bouts of depression in silence. The few sentences Fanny had written about herself worried Mary as much as detailed account of Godwin's troubles. What pain poor Fanny must have endured before confessing her misery!

When Percy came back from the lake, Mary and he talked about Godwin's and Fanny's problems. They decided to send her a gift, a small watch, to cheer her up.

Next, Claire announced she was pregnant. The Godwins would not be happy to hear that another unmarried daughter was pregnant. Byron did not welcome the news, either. He again made it clear his affection for Claire did not match hers for him. Mary and Shelley decided they would help take responsibility for the baby, and if need be, hide its existence from its grandparents.

The couple cancelled plans for a tour of Europe's waterways and left Geneva to return to England on August 29. Mary and Claire hurried to the spacious house Shelley leased near the village of Marlow, anxious to avoid the curious public which had spread gossip about them in the past. Percy went to London, and began another round of attempts to get his finances in order. When he returned, Mary informed him she would take care of their finances from then on, an idea Percy first considered amusing. But she proved herself more practical than he, and Percy soon learned to trust her judgment.

Another letter arrived from Fanny. "I depart immediately to

the spot from which I hope never to remove," Fanny wrote. It was clear she was threatening suicide.

Percy hurried to Wales, where Fanny was visiting relatives. But a newspaper account of a young woman who had committed suicide with an overdose of laudanum stopped him. He was too late. Fanny had been found clutching the bottle in her cold hand, a final note hinting at her suffering: "Perhaps to hear of my death will give you pain," she wrote, "but you will soon have the blessing of forgetting that such a creature ever existed ..."

Fanny did not finish the sentence. She had dutifully left out her name, a last attempt to prevent further scandal.

The shock paralyzed Mary; she was unable to rise from bed. Percy wrote a poem in Fanny's memory. When Mary recovered enough to write, she sent a letter to her father expressing her grief and condolence. Godwin had ignored her other letters. He chose to reply to this one, in a cold tone that must have brought scarce comfort: "I did indeed expect it," Godwin wrote. "I cannot but thank you for your strong expression of sympathy. I do not see, however, that that sympathy can be of any service to me; but it is best. My advice and earnest prayer is that you would avoid anything that leads to publicity.

"Go not to Swansea; disturb not the silent dead; do nothing to destroy the obscurity that she so much desired that now rests upon the event. It was, as I said, her last wish ..."

It was also Godwin's wish that his name not be smeared by the press. He wrote that the family was debating whether to claim that Fanny had gone to live with an aunt in Ireland. Godwin's worries may have been less selfish than they appear to be. If it was widely known that Fanny had killed herself, English authorities would not have allowed her proper burial. But the suicide became public knowledge soon after her funeral, along with the inevitable gossip that Fanny had been in love with Percy. Experience had taught the couple how to ignore the rumors.

Then, on December 12, 1816, newspapers reported that authorities had found "a respectable woman far advanced in pregnancy" drowned in the Serpentine river. Several days later the mail brought word that the woman was Percy's wife Harriet.

Mary and Percy went on long walks together, trying to piece the situation together. To their friends, Percy tried to appear in command of his emotions, but Mary knew Harriet's death had staggered him, as it had her. Then, despite Harriet's last wishes that their children be taken in by Westbrooks, Percy began trying to win custody of his and Harriet's children, Ianthe and Charles.

After Harriet's suicide the two lovers realized their own relationship had changed. They were now free to marry, and began making wedding plans.

William Godwin was delighted at the news. His quarrels with the couple were forgotten. The wedding took place on December 29, 1816, at St. Mildred's Church on Bread Street in London. The Godwins served as witnesses. William Godwin cast aside the criticisms of marriage which had once been a bedrock of his philosophy: "According to the vulgar ideas of the world, she is well-married, and I have great hopes the young man will make her a good husband," Godwin wrote. He soon opened up to Mary again and resumed his friendship with Percy. The newlyweds tried to conceal their dislike of Mrs. Godwin, but avoided staying long at the house on Skinner Street.

Mrs. Godwin, too, trumpeted the news that Mary was honorably married, and to the son of a noble family at that. "I now have the pleasure to announce that Mr. Godwin's daughter, Mary, has entered the marriage state with Mr. Percy Bysshe Shelley, eldest son of Sir Timothy Shelley, Baronet ...," she wrote a friend of the family.

Two weeks later, on January 13, 1817, Claire gave birth to a daughter she first named Alba, after Byron's nickname of Albe, but soon changed to Allegra.

Mary was relieved to be married. She spent the time she wasn't writing with little William, now a year old, and treated Allegra with as much love as if she were her own child. Their social life blossomed at Marlow. The became close friends with Leigh Hunt, editor of the literary journal *The Examiner,* and his wife Marianne. Hunt was a man who valued friends of genius more than money, for which he had to scrimp almost as hard as Godwin. He championed those writers he deemed worthy. In 1817, he wrote an essay titled "The Young Poets" that named Shelley, John Keats and John Reynolds Hamilton as the best of their generation.

Percy was grateful for Hunt's support and made arrangements to meet him. "I have not in all my intercourse with mankind experienced sympathy and kindness with which I have been so affected or which my whole being has so sprung forward to meet and to return. ... Let me talk with you as with an old friend," Shelley wrote.

Percy and Mary began to spend much of their free time at the Hunts' cottage, which the Hunts called the *Vale of Health*. Mary admired Marianne for her quick mind and cheerful nature. There was always a crowd, with the Hunt's five children adding to the hubbub. One of the guests was twenty-five-year-old John Keats. Keats, the son of a middle class family, never became close to the aristocrat Shelley, although Percy always admired his poetry.

Percy lost his battle for custody of his two children from his marriage with Harriet. He had met determined foes in the Westbrook family, which blamed him for her death. The English court noted Shelley's atheism when it gave custody to the Westbrooks. He was forbidden to even see Ianthe and Charles. "No words can express the anguish he felt when his older children were torn from him," Mary later wrote. Percy never saw Ianthe and Charles again.

The Shelleys used their work as an escape from pain. In addition to poems and novels, they also wrote pamphlets about the political upheavals in England at the time. In 1817, England had just finished a successful war against the French. Unemployment rose as veterans returned home, and riots broke out. The government suspended basic rights and clamped down on the press. The Shelleys condemned the government's actions. Most women stayed out of politics, but following the example of Mary Wollstonecraft, Mary did not hesitate to voice her views.

Both Mary and Percy did some of their most important work

Leigh Hunt praised Percy's poetry in his newspaper *The Examiner*

during this period. He wrote his longest poem, *The Revolt of Islam,* and several shorter poems. Mary finished *Frankenstein* in May with a burst of creative energy she later paid for with an extended depression. The novel initially met a cool reception from the first publishers she sent it to, despite Percy's attempts to persuade them of its merits.

On September 9, Mary gave birth to their second child, whom she named Clara. Mary was delighted that Clara was a healthy baby, but she suffered another bout of depression soon after the birth. Mary began to wonder about her mood swings. Why did melancholy and dread always follow her periods of happiness? Her guilt over the tragedy that opened the way for their marriage began to haunt her. She would feel haunted by

Harriet's death for the rest of her life, often interpreting misfortune as fate's way of punishing her.

Percy's financial troubles returned. He lent money to both Godwin and Leigh Hunt and complicated matters with his own spending sprees. Creditors hounded him constantly; he lost weight and fell asleep while trying to work.

Certainly things would be much better in Italy. At first, Mary doubted they could afford the move. She spent an evening working through their financial records and calculated it would take 1500 pounds. Weighing her concern for Shelley, and her own desire to leave England against more debt, she wrote to her husband in London: "You tell me the Italian sun will be the best physician. Be it so. But money, money, money!"

Claire also exasperated Mary. Percy pitied Claire, as did Mary, because of the shabby treatment she received from Lord Byron. Claire exploited their pity to draw closer to Percy. She began to demand her private time with Percy, away from Mary, as one of her "rights." When Claire announced that Byron had agreed to take custody of Allegra and support the child, and that she was in a hurry to meet Byron in Italy, the Shelleys decided that was reason enough to leave England.

Before they left, exciting news arrived from London. The Lackington publishing company accepted *Frankenstein*. She and Percy labored over the galley proofs in the months before their departure. The book was published on March 11, 1818, the same day they, along with their children, Claire, and Allegra, left for the Italy.

Little Deaths

Even three noisy babies and an ill-tempered Claire could not interfere with Mary's euphoric mood as the carriage rattled over the dusty French countryside. It was wonderful to be away from England with its never-ending gossip and hounding creditors. Surely, their life would begin anew when they reached ancient, sunny Italy. Mary and Percy read novels, poetry and lectures as they traveled. When the carriage broke a spring, she took the time to revel in the beautiful scenery, which included a view of the Alps and the Jura.

On their arrival in Milan, the Shelleys went house-hunting. They met frustration at first, failing to secure a gorgeous villa they fell in love with on the shores of Lake Como. They continued their search from temporary lodgings, while trying to unite Allegra with Byron. But Byron's coldness astounded them. He finally replied to Shelley's many letters with a heartless proposition—he would take custody of Allegra only on condition that Claire renounce all rights to the child and never see her again. The Shelleys urged Claire to reject Byron's proposal. Byron's latest display of cruelty left Claire depressed and angry, although she decided to accept the harsh terms.

Hoping that a change of scene would improve Claire's spirits, they traveled to the city of Pisa, where the sight of chained convicts doing roadwork under the glare of armed guards seemed barbaric to them. They traveled on to stay for a while with Maria Gisborne, an old family friend of the Godwins, in the port city of Livorno. Mary thought it an ugly little town, but she enjoyed the company of the older woman, to whom William Godwin had once proposed marriage. "We had no idea of spending a month here, but she had made it agreeable," Mary wrote of her friend. Her mother Mary Wollstonecraft had once been Mrs. Gisborne's tutor, and the lady delighted Mary with tales of the mother she had never known.

The heat and noise of the bustling little town depressed Mary. Word that Percy had found a little house on the wooded hills by the Baths of Lucca came as welcome news. Soon after they moved to the comfortable house, Mary wrote a letter describing its pleasures to Mrs. Gisborne. She contrasted its quiet splendor with Livorno's large streets: "It is strange ... after having been accustomed for a month to the tumult of the Via Grande, to come to this quiet scene where we hear no sound except the rushing of the river in the valley below," she wrote.

Percy, too, enjoyed the rides along the hillside over the river, the mountain air, and the bracing swims. He and Mary sometimes had to nag one another to continue their work. Percy began collecting reviews of *Frankenstein*, some of which condemned the book, while others praised it. Even the bad notices did nothing to quell public interest, as Mary's strange tale entranced readers.

Shelley's health grew stronger, as did that of their two children, William and Clara. However, Claire's troubles surfaced again, as she heard news of the immoral environment of Byron's mansion where Allegra was growing up. Percy decided to intervene on her behalf, and he and Claire journeyed to see Byron in Venice.

While they were gone, the baby Clara fell ill with what at first seemed like diarrhea, which neighbors counseled Mary not to worry about. Clara had begun to fret and run a temperature when a letter arrived from Shelley asking for her and the children to join him.

Full of misgivings, Mary set out with her the children and a nursemaid. The coach carrying the party jolted along the dusty roads under merciless heat. Clara was desperately ill by the time they reached Este, a town outside of Venice where Byron had a villa. Percy, too, was sick, with what he thought was food poisoning, but when he discovered his daughter's condition he flew into a frenzy. Shelley did not trust the local doctors and insisted they go to Venice. In their panic, they left their passports at the villa, yet their fear and the baby's condition were so desperate that the startled customs officials let them through. By this time, Clara had fallen into a coma in her mother's arms.

After checking into an inn, Percy dashed off to find a doctor he knew. The doctor was out, and no one knew when he would return. Shelley went back to the hotel to find that Mary had summoned another doctor. The physicians offered a grim diagnosis. The baby was beyond help. Mary held Clara for hours, hoping desperately for some miraculous deliverance. Clara died at seven that evening.

Mary fought to control her grief, remembering the way sorrow had almost overpowered her after the death of her first baby. On September 26, the day of Clara's burial, she did not mention the event in her journal and insisted that she and Shelley visit their friends. She even interceded on Claire's behalf with Byron, who agreed to let Allegra return with them to their hotel.

Byron did extract a promise for his gesture. He asked Mary to transcribe his long poem *Malzeppa*. She agreed and put aside her own creative work when they returned to Byron's *Villa Cappucini*, laboring long hours over pages filled with Byron's hard-to-decipher writing.

Alone, her grief burst forth. Unlike Shelley, she did not easily give way to wild, outward expressions of emotion. Now she walked aimlessly through the house and garden. Mary's wanderings seemed as futile as those of the grieving ghosts in *Fantasmagoriana*. But she no longer took vicarious pleasure in fantasies of death and looked instead with dread upon an ancient castle behind the villa. What an aura of gloom those ruined grey walls cast over her spirit!

She wrote her father of her misery following Clara's death. Godwin's reply would have broken a heart of stone: "You should ... recognize that it is only persons of a very ordinary sort ... that sink long under a calamity of this nature," Godwin wrote. "We seldom indulge long in depression and mourning except when we think secretly that there is something very refined in it, and that it does us honour."

The stress Mary had suffered revealed itself the night before the family left for Rome. She and Percy were to dine with Byron. Sitting beside the lord at the table was his latest mistress, a baker's wife. Mary at first quietly refused to be seated with the woman. When her request for a different chair was ignored, her protests grew louder. She would not allow herself to be seated next to this "contemptible" woman, she said. The outburst surprised and embarrassed Percy, but she insisted he take her back to their hotel. Byron calmly observed the scene, neither embarrassed nor offended. Although Byron had few moral qualms, he claimed to find Mary's virtue admirable.

The trip to Rome settled the couple's nerves and helped them forget their recent sorrow. They strolled through the ancient sights of Rome where Percy discovered a cemetery more beautiful than any he had ever seen: "To see the sun shining on its bright grass, fresh ... with autumnal dews ... and hear the whispering of the wind among the leaves ... and to mark the tombs, mostly of women and young people who were buried there, one might, if one were to die, desire the sleep they seem to sleep," Shelley wrote.

The Shelleys busied themselves with their work. They sat for some portraits by Amelia Curran, an artist whom Mary had known since childhood. They eventually settled in a house Mrs. Gisborne had rented for them at the Baths of Lucca, where they had lived comfortably before. Mrs. Gisborne had urged them to live near her at Livorno, but Mary declined. She was concerned that the heat of the seaside city would damage

William's health.

A doctor Mary trusted warned that William was very frail, and advised the Shelleys to take him far from the smothering summers of Rome. They did not heed his warning. William seemed so bright and strong as he neared the middle of his fourth year. He was a beautiful and articulate child, who could switch from English to Italian in mid-sentence. Italian women would gather and dote over him as he slept: "His health and strength seemed to be perfect," Shelley wrote, "and his beauty, the silken transparence of his complection, the animation and deep blue color of his eyes were the astonishment of everyone."

Yet the transparency of William's skin was not the sign of good health that Shelley took it to be. It was one of the first symptoms of "Roman fever," a disease often deadly to small children.

William fell sick on June 2, 1819. The Shelleys summoned the doctor, who confirmed their fears. The little boy was critically ill. Mary felt helpless. It was as though some dark angel hovered over her, determined to snatch away all her loved ones. To her credit, Claire stepped in to act as William's nurse.

"William is in the greatest danger," Mary wrote Mrs. Gisborne. "We do not quite despair, yet we have the least possible reason to hope. Yesterday he was in the convulsions of death and he was saved from them—yet we dare not, must not hope."

For more than two days, Percy sat at William's bedside. Death came for little William on June 7, 1819. When it was over, the poet who could frighten himself into hysterics over ghost stories summoned all his self-control as he wrote the news of

This portrait of William Shelley was painted weeks before his death

his son's death to an old friend: "Yesterday, after an illness of only a few days, my little William died. There was no hope from the moment of the attack. You will be kind enough to tell all my friends, so that I need not to write to them."

The Shelleys buried William in the English cemetery Percy had found so beautiful. Both wanted to leave the city that now held such dreadful memories. They soon departed for Livorno, where Mrs. Gisborne had obtained them temporary quarters.

Percy always fought grief with work, and the house near Livorno had a beautiful study. In a tower encased by glass overlooking the sea, Percy worked on a drama in poetry called *The Cenci*. Yet Mary found no relief in any creative outlet. She was pregnant again, but could find no pleasure in the thought of another birth. How could she rejoice, after death had three times robbed her of her children? Would the next child be taken as well? She closed her journal of three years with despairing words: "Begun July 21st, 1816. Ended with my happiness June 7, 1819," Mary wrote. She wrote a friend that she would welcome the escape of her own death.

Despite their grief, the Shelleys prepared for Mary to get the best care possible when her fourth child was born. They moved to Florence, so she could be attended by Dr. Bell, who had first warned them of William's frailty. The city was home to many English residents and the lively conversations with her new friends helped ease her grief. On November 12 she gave birth to a healthy son they named Percy Florence.

An old friend of Mary's mother helped to further ease the tension in the household. Lady Mountcashell, a former student of Mary Wollstonecraft, arranged a position as governess for Claire. Mary quietly accepted Claire's absence as a blessing.

No sooner had Claire departed, however, than another houseguest arrived. Tom Medwin, a cousin who had attended school with Percy, came for a visit which eventually stretched over the winter. Medwin had served with the 24th Light Dragoons, a British Army unit in India. His military experience had inflated Medwin's ego. He fancied himself an adventurer and author. Medwin would interrupt the Shelleys in their own reading or writing to read aloud a long passage he had written. To make matters worse, he was a very poor poet, who took little notice of the pained expressions of his captive audience.

Medwin fell sick soon after his arrival and Mary nursed him.

While he recovered, Medwin took the opportunity to read some of his hosts' work. He discovered to his astonishment that both were brilliant writers, and for the first time realized the mediocrity of his own efforts. When he recovered, Tom Medwin was a much humbler guest.

Mary began work on a novel "illustrative of the manners of the Middle Ages in Italy" to be called *Castruccio*. Although never satisfied with the book, she later used much of her research in her second published novel *Valperga*.

Soon, two of Medwin's friends arrived. Edward Williams had attended Eton at the same time as Shelley, and had met Medwin in the army. He had saved his companion Jane from an abusive marriage, and the unmarried couple now lived as man and wife, along with their two children. Both Shelleys took to Edward immediately, who shared much of their philosophy and was an amateur painter.

It took longer for them to warm to Jane, whose devotion to her traditional role tried Mary's patience. She actually expected Mary to trade recipes with her! But Mary eventually realized Jane had her own talents, which included playing the guitar and singing. Mary decided that Jane was at least admirable for being trustworthy and, over time, the two became close friends and confidantes.

Shelley and Edward Williams shared a love for sailing, despite the fact that Shelley could not swim. It was a passion they shared with another newfound friend, Edward John Trelawny, whom they had met through Byron.

Trelawny was a handsome, dark-haired Cornish adventurer,

an amiable man and excellent storyteller. Six feet tall, he had joined the Royal Navy at the age of thirteen, fought in the war against the French, commanded a privateer—a vessel authorized for acts of plunder against the enemy—and had settled briefly in India, where he met Edward Williams. He was so well-muscled that Mary thought he looked like Hercules.

The men decided to look for a house near a body of water where they could sail. Not thrilled with the idea of yet another move, Mary occupied herself with the attempt to sell her second novel *Valperga*. One English publisher had already rejected it. She sent it to her father, asking him to intervene in her behalf. Godwin declared *Valperga* a better book than *Frankenstein*. Mary told her father he could keep the profits on the book if he found it a publisher, an offer he quickly accepted. While she awaited news from Godwin, the men looked for a house on the Gulf of Spezia.

In the midst of the activity, a messenger arrived with terrible news. An epidemic of typhus had struck the convent where Byron had placed Allegra. The child was dead. Mary ran weeping to her bed. She felt the curse had again caught up with her. In fact, it was a curse shared by many nineteenth century families, in a time when infant and child deaths were common.

The Shelleys did not want to tell Claire of Allegra's death in Pisa. Her feelings of anger toward Byron had deepened, and they were afraid she would attempt to harm him. They waited until a house had been found on the gulf, then asked Claire to come for a visit. When they told her the news Claire raved an entire night, blaming Byron in one breath and herself the next.

Then a strange calm seized her. She asked the Shelleys to request a portrait of her daughter and a lock of her hair and quietly returned to her job.

After Claire left, a feeling of dread descended on Mary. She had recently discovered she was pregnant again, and for once wished Claire had stayed, so she could offer her companionship and solace. Perhaps fueled by her depression over Claire's departure, Mary began to feel a sense of dread in the house. The *Casa Magni,* built next to the bay, looked more like a grim fortress than a home. On stormy days the waves beat against the house, and Mary could not shake the fear that further misfortune awaited her within the damp walls.

The Man Behind Shelley

Mary wrote in her journal that the endless crashing of the waves against the lower walls of *Casi Magni* was the most melancholy sound on earth. But Percy loved the house and even discussed making it their permanent home. He thought that Mary's depression was due to her new pregnancy, which was reviving memories of her three dead children.

But soon the other inhabitants began to have forebodings of imminent disaster. One afternoon, Jane Williams watched Percy walk across the terrace, trailed by someone whose features she couldn't make out. Who was following Percy? When the pair took a few more steps, the light fell on the face of the second man. It was also the face of Percy! Jane shivered in the sunlight as the phantom Percy disappeared.

She raced to tell Mary. Mary, although willing to use the supernatural in her tales, was more skeptical in her daily life. Surely, a trick of the light had fooled her friend.

Claire arrived on June 6, 1822. Three days later, Mary suffered a miscarriage, followed by hemorrhaging. For hours she lingered close to death. For once, it was Percy who kept his wits, insisting, over the objections of Claire and Jane, that Mary be packed in ice. The bleeding eventually stopped.

Percy was not so cool-headed one night a week later, when a dream sent him shrieking from his bed. "In the middle of the night I was awoke by hearing him scream and come rushing into my room," Mary later wrote. "I was sure that he was asleep, and tried to wake him by calling on him, but he continued to scream, which inspired me with such a panic that I jumped out of bed and ran across the hall to Mrs. Williams room." Jane opened the door and tried to calm Mary as Edward Williams went to see what was the matter with Percy.

Shelley insisted that while he lay awake, he had seen a vision of Edward Williams and Jane entering his room. "Edward and Jane came into him; they were in the most horrible condition ..." Mary wrote, "their bodies lacerated, their bones starting through their skins, the faces pale, yet stained with blood; They could hardly walk, but Edward was the weakest, and Jane was supporting him."

Then Edward spoke: "Get up, Shelley. The sea is flooding the house, and it is all coming down." Then the scene changed, and Percy saw himself strangling Mary.

Although Mary called the incident a nightmare, Percy swore it was no dream. He said that he had not been asleep, and insisted the scream Mary heard was not his. He recalled another detail the next morning. He had walked onto the terrace and found himself staring at another Percy, just as Jane had seen the double vision in the same spot. "How long do you mean to be content?" Percy's double asked him.

Before she returned to Pisa, Claire also suffered nightmares of some terrible fate that would befall Percy. Perhaps Claire's fear fed Percy's, as it so often had before. Mary sometimes wondered how she could find any peace of mind in this lonely place, with her companions frightening one another, and the crashing waves and wind undermining her own battle against depression. If Percy was so convinced that the omens signaled danger for him, why did he risk the frequent sailing trips with Edward Williams? Percy and Williams were not skilled sailors and Edward Trelawny, for one, felt uncomfortable with their talk of taking their small boat, *Don Juan,* onto the Atlantic. He urged them to stay in the bay.

Trelawny also wondered about the way Percy flirted openly with Jane Williams, and that Mary seemed to take no notice. Percy had even written an affectionate poem about Jane. But Mary had never felt threatened by any woman who was not her intellectual equal. Percy had written poems to other women, describing them in terms of heavenly beauty. Later, however, stories of Percy's infidelities would bring Mary unhappiness.

The same day Byron's splendid *Bolivar* sailed into the bay, Leigh and Marianne Hunt arrived at Genoa. Percy made plans for him and Edward Williams to pick them up in the *Don Juan.* They planned to sail on June 24.

The men were ready to weigh anchor when Jane dashed down the beach to stop them. Mary had suffered a relapse, and was distraught at his leaving. When Percy went back to the house, Mary's misery moved him to postpone his voyage. But, after calming, she urged Percy to set sail. At dawn on July 1,

Mary thought *Casa Magni* was the most melancholy place on earth

he and Williams prepared to do so, but Mary again begged him not to go, called him heartless to leave her, even threatened to take Percy Florence with her to Pisa if he sailed. Shelley was baffled. She had so often nursed him through fits of self-induced hysteria, taken care of practical matters he would have neglected, applied common sense in tense situations. Now their roles had reversed. Mary had seemingly lost all reason, over what was only a simple errand.

Miserably, Mary relented and told Percy to set sail with Williams. She walked back to the hated house and returned to bed, where she tossed and trembled.

Several days later a note arrived from Percy. The Hunts would not return with him. Marianne was not well. Percy tried to cheer Mary with his bright tone. "How are you, my best Mary?" he wrote, and asked if she could bear to stay at the *Casa Magni* until the end of summer.

July 8, 1822, the day Percy and Williams had planned to return, was wild and stormy. Mary and Jane were sure the two sailors would postpone their voyage.

On July 12, a letter arrived from Leigh Hunt. He wrote that Percy and Williams had set sail on July 8, and that he was worried for their safety. Would they write him to ease his mind? Mary's heart sank.

Mary and Jane hired a coach and hurried to Livorno, where the Hunt's were staying. Hunt had still not seen Percy or Edwards since they set sail. Neither had Byron, or Trelawny, who suggested that they had gone off course and landed on another shore of the bay. Surely they would arrive in another day, perhaps two. Trelawny rode home with the women in the carriage, urging them not to worry.

But, on July 19, Trelawny found the bodies of Percy and Williams washed up on the shore. They had been under water so long only their clothes and possessions provided clues to their identities. Trelawny found a book of John Keats's poetry in Shelley's pocket, with the binding folded back. He had apparently been reading the book shortly before the boat went down.

Trelawny walked back to the *Casa Magni*. He tried to find words, but his voice failed him. Seeing the sorrow on his face, a maid broke into tears. He found Mary, Jane and Claire on the terrace, and still could not speak the words. It was Mary who finally spoke. "Is there no hope?" she asked. Trelawny shook his head. He turned and walked into the house, searching for a nursemaid for the Shelley and Williams children. When he saw Mary again, several hours later, he spoke to her of Shelley's greatness as a poet and man.

The exact circumstances of the wreck of the *Don Juan* were never settled. Sailors who crossed its path offered conflicting tales. One captain said he had turned his ship back toward shore because of the bad weather when he caught sight of Shelley's boat. It was heading straight for a fog bank that hung like a gray castle over the seas. The *Don Juan* vanished into the folds of fog as though passing behind a curtain.

Only three people were able to attend the hurried cremation that was required by Italian law—Byron, Trelawny and Hunt. They erected a funeral pyre, placed his body, along with the book Shelley had been reading, on the pyre. Then they put the torch to poet's remains. Byron, overcome with grief, waded into the surf and swam out to his own ship. Trelawny poured wine, salt and frankincense into the blaze. When the fire shot up, he pulled Percy's heart from the flames.

Trelawny wanted the heart as a keepsake for Mary. She had a silver box made and kept it until her death. Percy's ashes were buried beside his son in Rome in the cemetery he had thought so beautiful.

Shelley's critics refused to let him die without one more attack. One article began, "Shelley, the writer of some infidel poetry has been drowned; *now* he knows whether there is a God or no."

The cruelty of Percy's enemies shocked Mary. In coming

months, she would discover that the world could also be a cold place for widows. But for the present she was full of grief."You are free, my Shelley," she wrote shortly after his funeral, "while I, your poor chosen one, am left to live as I may."

Mary's sorrow over Percy's death was made worse by her belief the world had never recognized his genius. She staggered through daily life as dazed as if someone had struck her a physical blow, remembering things she had meant to tell him, and tormenting herself over the times she might have treated him coldly. Harriet's ghost also lingered with her at times; Mary considered Shelley's death by drowning, the same fate Harriet had suffered, a dreadful irony.

"I never saw such a scene—nor wish to see such another," Byron wrote after seeing Mary at Pisa. When Jane and her children left for England, depriving her of the only friend who shared her plight, Mary wrote to Maria Gisborne: "Well, here is my story,the last story I shall have to tell. All that might have been bright in my life is now despoiled. I shall live to improve myself, to take care of my child, and render myself worthy to join him. ... I rest now, but soon I must leave Italy, and then there is an end to all but despair."

When Percey's father Sir Timothy abruptly stopped the allowance he had been paying her husband, she wrote requesting that he at least provide support for Percy Florence. For months, she received no reply.

She began preparing a posthumous volume of Shelley's poems. As she recovered, she earned the respect of all who knew her by rarely talking of her grief, though she still wrote of it in her letters and journal. She battled her internal demons alone, trying not to burden others with her own misfortunes.

Claire left Italy a few weeks after Shelley's death. For the rest of their lives, they would see each other only on occasional visits, although they continued to write regularly. Claire first went to visit her brother Charles in Vienna, where she worked as a tutor, and spent the rest of her life working as a tutor or governess in Austria, Italy, France and Russia.

When the Hunts invited her to move with them to Genoa, Mary was grateful to go. Pisa had become a haunted city for her, filled everywhere with memories. Yet life with the Hunts was far from easy. Marianne Hunt's doctor had told her she had cancer, a diagnosis that turned out to be incorrect. The doctor's error shattered Marianne's cheerful disposition. She talked endlessly about her symptoms. The Hunts were slovenly house-keepers, leaving their furniture caked in dust and their kitchen stacked with greasy, unwashed dishes and pots. Their children, denounced by Byron as "little Yahoos," made a game of teasing Percy Florence. Mary waited until Percy was in bed before beginning her editing work. Even then, it was nearly impossible to work in the Hunts' crowded house.

Finally, Sir Timothy Shelley wrote demanding full custody of Percy Florence before he would contribute to the boy's upkeep. Mary was shocked at the suggestion, and was further outraged when Byron said she should accept Sir Timothy's offer. Byron, while always kind toward her, had also disappointed her by refusing to honor his financial commitment to Hunt's newspaper *The Liberal*, which died because of lack of funds. Mary felt herself growing apart from her old friend, who soon left for Greece with Trelawny, although she would continue to admire his intellect and his poetry.

Mary began to consider returning to England. Although she had loved Italy, her friends were leaving and her situation was not improving. Maybe if she and little Percy were closer to Sir Timothy the old man would change his mind about supporting his grandson. When Godwin wrote asking her to come home, she decided to return. At least in England she could be near Jane Williams. On July 25, 1823, a year after Shelley's death, Mary and Percy Florence left for England.

False Hearts

Mary had not expected her return to England to attract much notice. In Italy, most of her friends had considered her Shelley's wife and widow. "But lo, and behold, I found myself famous," Mary wrote to Leigh Hunt on her return to England. *Frankenstein* was still popular.

Her literary success helped revive her spirits. Mary continued to directly address Shelley's spirit in her journals, and, surprisingly for one not reared in a religious background, looked forward to their reunion in the afterlife. But the respect of the public and literary establishment was a good antidote for mourning.

Mary found her fame to be a two-sided coin. On the one hand, many people revered her talent and thought *Frankenstein* to be proof that all the early prophecies of her inherited genius had been correct. Many admirers elevated her even further, considering her the perfect model of a Romantic heroine — brilliant, beautiful, independent and creative. Yet her critics considered the novel to be blasphemous and immoral. A London "morals society" handed out pamphlets in the streets, warning fathers to keep their families away from the popular play based on *Frankenstein.*

Mary enjoyed fame throughout England, Europe and even America. Yet she discovered, like her father before her, that fortune did not always follow fame. Her battle for financial security dulled the pleasure her celebrity might have brought her.

The more liberal members of the aristocracy welcomed her into their homes, and she became friends with England's best-known writers. But she occasionally suffered unexpected snubs. Rebuke could come when she least expected it. One hostess, for example, introduced her to the famed feminist Lucy Aiken, an admirer of Wollstonecraft and Godwin. Aiken stunned Mary and onlookers by turning her back on Mary and refusing to speak to her.

Mary's novel, *Valperga,* written in Italy before Percy's death, was published in 1823, the year Mary returned to England. A romance set in the Italy of the Middle Ages, the young heroine is named Euthanasia, Greek for "good death." Euthanasia defies conventional beliefs, loves wisdom and liberty, and tries to overthrow princes and priests in her struggle for equality. Her lover is Castruccio, a man much like Victor Frankenstein, who destroys all that is good in his character in his pursuit of power.

The book did not sell well. Eager for another horror story, the public was disappointed. Critics gave the book good notices, but *Valperga* sold slowly.

Mary began work on *The Last Man,* a novel based on the now

common science fiction theme of "the last man on Earth." She was determined it would be her masterpiece, with enough intellectual content to please the critics and with events dreadful enough to satisfy a public clamoring for more horrors.

Mary had little success in her first efforts toward ensuring Shelley his position of greatness in English literature. She made the rounds of publishers, attempting to interest one in publishing the huge body of Shelley's unpublished writings. But most editors did not share her view of her late husband's gifts. They considered him a little-known poet who had died young. Did they not often die young? Percy Bysshe Shelley had run his race, in their opinion, and it had not amounted to much.

Mary was determined not to let Shelley's poetry go unpublished. Finally, a friend of Leigh Hunt's approached Mary with a proposal to publish an edition of Shelley's poems. He, along with other admirers, paid for the publication. Hunt wrote an introduction. The volume sold well and generated unprecedented praise. "Shelley has celebrity, even popularity now," Mary wrote, angry that it took Shelley's death to make the literary world reconsider his talent.

Sir Timothy Shelley, who had reluctantly granted Mary a small allowance when she returned to England, was infuriated at the book's publication. He wanted the world to forget his scandalous son. He threatened to stop further payments if Mary did not stop distributing the poetry. Mary had no choice but to suppress the publication after only 300 copies had been sold.

Mary was determined not to be thwarted by the stubborn nobleman, but she could not openly defy him either. Her son's future depended on financial support from Sir Timothy. Mary bided her time. She was young. She could champion Shelley's poetry after Sir Timothy passed on.

In the meantime, she labored over her own work. Her family and friends expressed doubts when they found she was turning out another book on a macabre theme. Godwin thought *Valperga* a better book than *Frankenstein*. Claire agreed with her step-father: "You could write upon metaphysics, politics, jurisprudence, astronomy, mathematics—all those highest subjects which men taunt us with being incapable of treating—and surpass them," Claire wrote. Mary replied that she needed to earn a living with her writing. She had to entertain her audience as well as enlighten them. As for proving herself the equal of male writers, had she not done as much by writing a book so terrifying that the public refused at first to believe it could have been penned by a woman?

While working on *The Last Man*, Mary made an unsettling discovery. Writing, once a joy, had become work. "My imagination is dead, my genius lost, my energies sleep," she wrote. She had to force herself through her daily writing sessions.

She toiled throughout the spring of 1824. Then, on May 14, she suffered a severe depression. The next day's news made Mary believe she had experienced a premonition. Lord Byron, who had sided with the rebels in Greece's revolt against the Ottoman Turks, had died. She wrote a tribute to him in her journal, calling Byron "that resplendent spirit whom I loved." When church officials refused to allow Byron's body to rest in Westminster Abbey, his survivors decided to bury Byron in his

Edward Trelawny lived with the Shelley's that fateful summer of 1822

family's vault. His funeral procession marched by her house in Kentish Town, a small village near London.

"He could hardly be called a friend," she wrote Trelawny, "but connected with him in a thousand ways, admiring his talents & with all his faults feeling affection for him, it went to my heart when ... the hearse that contained his lifeless form, a form of beauty which in life I often delighted to behold, passed my window ..."

Her premonition reinvigorated Mary's belief that she could see into the future with her fiction. She had already written about characters based on herself and Shelley. Mary added a character much like Byron to *The Last Man*, making him the ruler of a 21st century England. She felt she had reclaimed her creative fire. "I feel my powers again—& this is of itself happiness," she wrote. "The eclipse of winter is passing from my mind."

Mary had moved to Kentish Town to be near Jane Williams. The young widows took comfort in talking about their shared past. Mary also encouraged Jane's courtship with Percy's old friend Thomas Jefferson Hogg. She mentioned Jane frequently in her letters to Jeff. She did so despite her reservations about whether Jane and Hogg would be good for one another.

Only slowly did Mary realize that Jane's friendship was not what it seemed. One of the first signs came during a holiday the two took together during the summer of 1826. Mary had a pleasant time, but it was all ruined at the end of the trip when she overheard Jane exclaim "Thank God, it is over!" The thought that her friend of so many years thought so little of her company sickened Mary.

When Jane and Hogg did marry in 1827, they proved to be an inconsiderate, cruel and perfectly matched pair of gossips. The newlyweds soon began to undermine Mary's reputation. Shelley had told Jane things he had never told Mary, Jane said, had written songs for her and, in the weeks before his death, had promised her his undying love. Hogg believed that Shelley and Jane had been lovers and worked to spread the stories.

Mary was shocked at their duplicity. Her faith in her friend was shattered, and she began to doubt the sincerity of everyone she had once trusted. She could think nothing else for weeks, including her work. Mary wrote Trelawny about the Hoggs' treachery. He replied that he had never liked Jane from the time he met her.

Mary sought the advice of one of her new friends, Thomas Moore. Moore was one of the most celebrated writers in England and a long-time friend of her father. Moore told Mary she should not allow her pain to torment her in private. She should confront Jane.

She followed his advice and wrote a harsh letter. Shamed by the knowledge that Mary had found her out, Jane could not bring herself to repeat the charge. She instead wrote of the misery Mary's stinging words had caused her. But Mary refused to let herself be deceived again. She demanded an apology. Jane finally realized that she was trapped by her deceit and begged Mary to forgive her.

Mary forgave her, but the damage had been done. Jane's betrayal instilled a deep distrust in Mary that would last the rest of her life. She wrote of her disillusionment years later: "I am copying Shelley's letters. Great God, what a thing is life! In one of them he says 'the curse of this life is that what we have once known we cannot cease to know ...' Life is not all ill till we wish to forget. Jane first inspired me with that miserable feeling, staining past years as she did—taking the sweetness from memory and giving it instead a serpent's tooth."

"Proof Against Man & Woman"

After the episode with Jane, Mary approached life with more determination and less idealism. In 1826, when Charles, Percy and Harriet's son, died, leaving Percy Florence as the heir to Sir Timothy's title and fortune, Mary lost no time in writing to her father-in-law and asking him to provide adequate funds to properly educate his new heir. Sir Timothy had no choice but to agree. His heir must be properly trained. Still refusing to meet with her, he dealt with Mary through his lawyers. They worked out an arrangement which increased Percy Florence's tuition to cover tuition and books, but left Mary responsible for paying his room and board. In addition, Mary was to allow Percy Florence to visit Field Place three times a year. During his stays, Sir Timothy warned the boy not to follow in his father's footsteps.

The Last Man, published in 1826, startled readers and critics alike. The story takes place in the 21st century, and describes a plague that wipes out the entire population of earth, except for the narrator. It also accurately predicted future threats. The global extinction of the race, so awful an idea to readers of the

19th century, has since become a realistic possibility. Mary even named the rulers of England the Windsors, the name of the current royal family.

But most of the critics of the time were not ready for science fiction. The book received some favorable notices, but many were hostile. One literary gazette called it "sickening," another accused it of "stupid cruelties," yet another example of a "diseased imagination and ... polluted taste." *Monthly Review* compared it unfavorably with *Frankenstein*.

Mary's ardent readers, however, delighted in the book and she earned a handsome six hundred pounds in the first year, and one hundred pounds each year for five years. Like all popular writers, Mary had learned to give readers what they wanted.

Her readership extended to France, and in the late spring of 1828 she traveled to Paris to lecture. But shortly after arrival, she came down with smallpox. The disease often disfigured people and she made a joke of it, calling herself "the monster." She cancelled her lectures, but did not hesitate to visit her friends even while wearing her "mask." "It was rather droll to play the part of an ugly person for the first time in my life, yet it was amusing to be told—or rather not to be told but to find that my face was not all my fortune." A visit to the sunny shore of France erased all signs of the disease.

However, it was not Mary's face that her old friend Edward John Trelawny found most changed, but her attitude. He asked to write a book on the life of Shelley. Mary refused. Sir Timothy would be infuriated by such a book, and she would not allow Trelawny to endanger her son's livelihood. Besides, Trelawny had only known Shelley for four months!

Trelawny returned to Italy in a sour mood. He continued to snipe at her, and would write unflattering descriptions in his letters, painting her as a woman who looked pretty enough at night parties, but haggard by day. In fact, Mary was barely thirty, and still quite beautiful. She decided to try to patch things up with Trelawny by helping to find a publisher for his memoirs *The Adventures of a Younger Son.*

Trelawny took her help as a sign she was attracted to him. He speculated that they were destined to be together in one of his letters. "I should not wonder if fate, without our choice, united us; and who can control his fate?"

Mary attempted to gently reject his advances, saying she could not give up her lovely name. "Mary Shelley shall be written on my tomb—and why? I cannot tell, except that it is so pretty a name that though I were to preach to myself for years, I never should have the heart to get rid of it."

But Trelawny persisted. "I was more delighted with your resolve not to change your name than with any other portion of your letter," he wrote. "Trelawny too is a good name and sounds as well as Shelley."

Mary realized that nothing would do but to set him straight.

"My name will never be Trelawny," she answered back in her next letter. "You belong to womankind in general, and Mary Shelley will never be yours."

Trelawny and many others thought Mary was content to play the role of Shelley's widow for the rest of her life. They were mistaken. Mary repeatedly attempted to find someone to share her life. But after living with Shelley, she could not stand the thought of marrying anyone with an intellect inferior to her own. That was the mistake her own father had made, she thought, when he hastily married Mrs. Godwin after her mother's death.

Then, too, another fear nested in the back of her mind. She had heard often how her mother Mary Wollstonecraft had wasted her affections on the scoundrel Gilbert Imlay. She did not want to make a similar mistake. She turned down many suitors, including the well-known playwright and actor John Howard Payne. Ironically, Payne later tried to play the matchmaker between his friend, the American writer Washington Irving, the author of "The Legend of Sleepy Hollow," and Mary. She did admire Irving, but his personality was too much like her own. They were both so reserved they never developed a close relationship.

In addition to her books, Mary also wrote articles and encyclopedia entries to increase her income between books. In 1830, she published *Perkin Warbeck*, a tale about a man who wages a battle for the English throne, on the grounds that it is rightfully his by birth. Perkin Warbeck was a real historical character. He had confessed to being an imposter before being executed, but Mary believed he had been the heir to the crown, as he first claimed. After her fictional Warbeck dies, his widow Katherine works for the education of her son, whom she considers the crown prince. Katherine's efforts, of course, were modeled on her own in behalf of Percy Florence. The book was not a success. It sold for one hundred and fifty pounds and brought her little profit thereafter. "Poor Perkin Warbeck," she lamented to her publisher.

Despite her literary set-back, Mary accomplished one of her longstanding goals in 1832, when she enrolled Percy Florence in the boys school, Harrow. She had to leave London so that he could live with her as a day student. She hated to leave the city behind, and hated Harrow as well, but made the best of it. "To go and live at pretty Harrow," she told Maria Gisborne, "with my boy, who improves each day, and is everything I could wish is no bad prospect."

Working in a place which depressed her, Mary nonetheless enjoyed success with her next book *Lodore*, published in 1835. The story paralleled her own life. Thirty-four year old Lord Lodore marries sixteen-year-old Cornelia Santerre, a woman much like Shelley's first wife Harriet. Cornelia's mother breaks up the couple, and causes her to neglect her daughter Ethel. Lord Lodore kidnaps Ethel and takes her to the American wilderness. Lodore is killed on a trip to England, and Ethel marries. She and her young husband suffer scorn similar to that experienced by Mary and Percy. Eventually, Cornelia escapes her mother and is happily reunited with her daughter and son-in-law.

Reviewers praised *Lodore* and sales climbed for over two years. With her pen shoring up her funds, Mary was able to use the proceeds to board her son with a tutor when he was sixteen.

Finally, Mary was free of the money worries that had plagued her since she first eloped with Percy. But the years of struggling and suffering had changed her. The romantic writer, who wanted to change the world with her work, now wrote for money. Her painful life had toughened her. "I am now proof, as Hamlet says, against man and woman," she wrote.

Words In Stone

William Godwin died in his eightieth year on April 7, 1836. He spent his last five days in bed, and Mary sat up with him every night. "His last moment was very sudden," Mary wrote an old family friend. "Mrs. Godwin and I were both present. He was dozing tranquilly, when a slight rattle called us to his side, his heart ceased to beat, and all was over."

Despite the hurt that remained over the way her father had treated her while Shelley was alive, Mary had protected her father in his old age. She helped him find new lodgings after he was evicted from Skinner Street, and successfully petitioned Parliament to grant him an allowance for his literary achievements. After his death, her restraint and cool-headedness in settling his estate would not have surprised the man who rebuked his daughter for "indulging" her grief when Clara had died. Godwin was buried on April 7 in St. Pancras graveyard, beside the grave of Mary Wollstonecraft.

Mary also saw to it that Mrs. Godwin was well-provided for during her years as a widow. She even took it on herself to ask others for favors, a task she always despised, on the part of her step-mother. She asked Charles Lamb—now a rich and titled man—for an allowance for Mrs. Godwin. The stipend was granted, and Mrs. Godwin lived comfortably until her death in 1841.

In the fall of 1836, Percy Florence began attending classes at Trinity College, Cambridge. Greatly relieved that his time at Harrow were over, Mary moved to London and took a house on Park Street. Her books had made her popular, and she became a frequent visitors to literary teas of the publisher John Murray, and at parties in the homes of wealthy admirers.

She was also hard at work on her new book. The heroine of *Falkner*, Elizabeth Raby, was, much like Mary, "lovely from her birth." Elizabeth, an orphan, is adopted by Falkner, a wild and passionate man determined to seek justice for the oppressed. Falkner who, much like Shelley, lives with guilt over the fate of his first wife, Alithia, who had drowned trying to escape him.

Elizabeth deeply loves her stepfather. She also loves Alithia's son Gerard, and when Falkner is imprisoned for Alithea's murder, Gerard and Elizabeth work to clear his name. After they prove Falkner's innocence, Elizabeth and Gerard marry and live near Falkner. The ending of *Falkner* neatly resolves problems that had proven unresolvable in Mary's own life. In the end, for example, Elizabeth keeps the affection of both her husband and her father, a happiness that had been denied Mary.

Writing the story was difficult work, and shortly before finishing the book, in October of 1836, Mary suffered an emotional and physical breakdown that she did not recover from until January. "My race is run," Mary had written in her diary

Mary Shelley's novels were popular during the 1830s and 1840s

the year before. *Falkner* would be her last major work of fiction.

Mary continued working on behalf of Shelley's poetic legacy, and her hard work was beginning to pay off. But, as always, her efforts exposed her to criticism. When she brought out an 1839 edition of *Queen Mab,* the publisher advised her to omit the dedication to Harriet for fear it would resurrect old scandals. But both the Hoggs and Trelawny condemned Mary for the omission. They assumed she did not want any mention of her former rival. Jealousy probably motivated them to see the worst in her actions. Yet their criticism hurt and puzzled Mary. "I much disliked the leaving out of any of *Queen Mab,*" she wrote. "I disliked it still more than I can express and I even wish I had resisted to the last; but when I was told that certain portions would injure the copyright of all the volumes to the publisher, I yielded."

Sir Timothy fumed over Mary's defiance of his wishes regarding publication of Shelley's work. Yet with Sir Timothy in his eighties and still enjoying good health, Mary realized she would have to defy his request or risk the chance that Percy's poetry would be lost for all time. When she also published a collection of his lyric poems, Sir Timothy insisted that it not include a biography of Shelley. Mary managed, however, to score a sly victory by inserting lengthy biographical notes on the poems. She also published a collection of Shelley's prose works in 1840, along with *History of a Six Weeks Tour*, a book she wrote describing her travels with Shelley after they eloped. Sir Timothy grumbled and cursed his daughter-in-law, but in the end he left Percy Florence's allowance intact.

Percy Florence sided with his mother in her conflicts with his grandfather. Although he had little of his parent's literary talent, he had grown to appreciate what they had accomplished with their writing, and as he matured he remained close to his mother. In 1840, the year he turned twenty-one, Percy Florence and his friends invited Mary to join them for a tour of Europe. She protested at first, arguing that a woman in her forties would be out of place among a group of young men. But Mary had many admirers, and Percy Florence's friends were among them. They insisted, and as the trip progressed she was glad she had done so.

Among the happiest moments of the journey came when she visited Geneva. She looked upon the villas where she and her young friends had traded ghostly tales, and where she had dreamed of Frankenstein and his Monster before her nineteenth birthday. "There ... stood *Diodati*; and our humble dwelling, *Maison Chapius*, nestled close to the lake below," she wrote. "There were the terraces, the vineyards, the upward path threading them, the little port where our boat lay moored. I could mark and recognize a thousand slight peculiarities, familiar objects then—forgotten since ... Was I the same person who had lived there, the companion of the dead?"

Mary and her young friends enjoyed themselves so much that they returned to the continent on another trip in 1841. She wrote an account of their adventures, *Rambles in Germany and Italy*. It was her last book.

Sir Timothy died in April of 1844 at the age of ninety, the ancient patriarch "falling from the stalk like an overgrown flower," as Mary described it to Hogg. After settling the debts against the estate, Mary discovered that Sir Timothy had left a smaller inheritance than she had expected. But it was enough to secure a comfortable life for herself and her son. Percy Florence was now Sir Percy, a member of the English aristocracy.

Many of Mary's struggles had ended. In 1848, Sir Percy Florence introduced her to the woman who would become his wife, Jane St. John. Mary's assessment of the highborn young woman, herself a widow, was far more generous than any Mary had received from her own in-laws. "She is a prize indeed in the lottery being the best & sweetest thing in the world," Mary told a friend. Jane was equally fond of Mary. She described her as slim and young looking, though by then Mary was past fifty. Jane also complimented Mary's grace and her deep-set, expressive eyes.

Mary spent a great deal of time with the couple after they married, traveling with them from estates at Chester Square to Field Place. She had finally reached a state of tranquility, caring little for fame or the world's opinions. Jane was very protective of her mother-in-law, once chasing Claire from her door after Claire had unleashed one of her tirades against Mary. "She has been the bane of my life ever since I was two!" Mary confided to Jane.

Mary worried about Jane's health, which sometimes suffered in the dampness of Field Place. In 1850, she went with the couple to Nice in France, enjoying a beautiful summer much like those in her youth. After returning to England, the couple returned to Field Place and Mary went to the house she owned in London. Sir Percy and Lady Jane worried about Mary in her house alone. Despite her apparent vigor, they thought she had tired too quickly during their vacation.

In mid-January, they visited Mary and found her in bed, half-paralyzed. Mary calmly informed them that she was dying, and that she wanted to do so in her own house.

During her last struggle, Mary showed a faith that might have surprised Shelley, and that was contrary to Godwin's philosophy. "I shall join your father soon," she told Sir Percy, "so I do not care what is done with my body."

Mary Wollstonecraft Godwin Shelley's heart stopped in the early morning hours of February 1, 1851. She was fifty-four.

One of Mary's last wishes was to be buried near the bodies of her parents. But the area around the once-beautiful St. Pancras graveyard had deteriorated into one of the ugliest neighborhoods in London. Lady Jane was determined not to let Mary be buried there. "It would have broken my heart to let her loveliness wither in such a dreadful place," Lady Jane wrote later. She decided that the bodies of Godwin and Wollstonecraft should be exhumed and reburied with their daughter in the better-kept cemetery at St. Peters Church in Bournemouth.

The rector at St. Peters at first refused to allow the burials. The writings of all three still infuriated traditional-minded people. He would not have the three rebels against convention laid to rest in his cemetery. But a determined Lady Jane forced his hand when she appeared at the cemetery behind a hearse carrying the three coffins. She declared she would remain at the iron gates of the graveyard until they were admitted. The rector realized that the spectacle of a noblewoman keeping a stubborn vigil at the cemetery's entrance would cause even more scandal than the burials themselves. He reluctantly allowed the hearse and carriage through.

The grave diggers worked quickly. Even so, night had fallen by the time the bodies were lowered into the graves.

There was no religious service. Instead, at Sir Percy's request, an Anglican clergyman struggled to read one of the last passages Mary had written in her journal:

> God and good angels guard us! Surely this world, stored outwardly with shapes and influences of beauty and good, is peopled in its intellectual life by myriads of loving spirits that mould our thoughts to good, influence beneficially the course of events, and minister to the destiny of man. Whether the beloved dead make a portion of this company, I dare not guess, but that such exist I feel—far off, when we are worldly, evil, selfish; drawing near and imparting joy and sympathy when we rise to noble thoughts and disinterested action. Such surely gather round one on such an evening, and make part of that atmosphere of love, so hushed, so soft, on which the soul reposes and is blest.

The rector again protested when Sir Percy and Lady Jane

insisted that some mention of the three authors' works be placed on the graves. He eventually agreed for Godwin's stone to be inscribed as "Author of Political Justice." Mary Wollstonecraft was again laid to rest with the carved phrase that had meant so much to the young Mary Godwin, "Author of a Vindication of the Rights of Women."

The rector refused any memorial mentioning Mary's best-known work. No gravestone in his cemetery would bear the inscription "Author of Frankenstein." A simple plaque placed near Mary Shelley's grave describes her only as "Author" and "Wife of the Poet."

Notes

Page 10: Some of Mary Wollstonecraft's friends shunned her after she married Godwin, but most of her circle considered the marriage a union of genuis. Mary Wollstonecraft continued to work, writing a novel called *The Wrongs of Women; or Maria*, which called for an end to the double standard of sexual conduct for men and women, and urged greater freedom in divorce laws.

Page 17: The writers in Godwin's circle at Skinner Street often wrote stories for Mary. Godwin wrote about a girl and her father visiting the grave of her mother, in which he describes a "Great Spirit" which protects her even in the midst of death. Mary Lamb published a story about a girl who learns to write her name by tracing her mother's name on a tombstone, just as Godwin had taught Mary. The girl overcomes her morbid attachment to the grave when her Uncle James, an officer in the Navy, persuades her that her mother would have wanted her to look beyond death to her own bright promise.

Page 22: Percy Shelley sometimes struck his friend Hogg as both a genius and a maniac. Once, while crossing a bridge, Shelley seized a baby from the arms of its startled mother, and began to eagerly question the infant about its existence before its birth, in order to make a point in an argument the two were having about spirtuality.

Page 24: Post-obit lenders like those who provided the money for Shelley's "loans" to Godwin generally charged a fee of three times the sum borrowed, to be paid upon the receipt of the borrower's inheritance.

Page 25: Harriet Westbrook Shelley may have been more intelligent than the intellectuals of Skinner Street knew. She was in awe in the company of well-known artists and writers. Harriet wrote letters describing Godwin as a man of genius who physically resembled the Greek philosopher Socrates, and having carefully studied the features of Mary Wollstonecraft in her portrait, said that she looked like a woman who dared to think for herself.

Page 32: One of the few possessions Mary carried with her was a box of papers which contained her letters and her earliest attempts at fiction, including the never-finished novel *Hate*. In Paris, she showed the contents of the box to Shelley, who encouraged her to finish her novel. But the box was lost and never recovered. There is no surviving manuscript of *Hate*.

Page 47: The strange weather of the summer of 1816 was created by the explosion of a distant volcano, Mount Timboro, located near Bali in the East Indies. Mount Timboro's eruption killed 56,000 people and blew millions of tons of ash into the atmosphere, blocking the sunlight and playing havoc with weather throughout the Northern hemisphere.

Pages 51-52: One reason few people remember John Polidori's book *The Vampyre* was the sucesss of Bram Stoker's *Dracula*, published in 1897. Many people had told tales of vampires before anyone wrote about them, so it is not surprising that only the best of the written stories have survived until this day. The rivalry of vampire novelists illustrates another strength of *Frankenstein*. No writer could "top" Mary's tale, because she based it not on folklore, but on an original idea.

Page 56: Frankenstein's Monster, as described in the book is—unlike most of the stage and movie versions—mentally brilliant and physically agile. In fact, he is at his diabolical best when convincing Frankenstein to look past his own conscience and to forget his creation's murders as he labors to create another such being.

Pages 64-65: Godwin may have urged Shelley to marry his daughter in a meeting they had shortly after Harriet's death. Given Godwin's desperate scrounging for money, the fact that Sir Timothy might be obliged to lift his ban on his son's borrowing could have played a part in Godwin's support for the marriage.

Pages 70-71: Percy clearly enjoyed reading Mary's reviews more than she did. She did not like talking about her work during or after writing it, preferring instead to concentrate all her energy into the project at hand during specified hours of the day, and to spend her leisure time talking about art, music or the work of other writers.

Page 77: Through another friend, the Shelleys met a person who held them both in thrall. He was the Greek Prince Mavrocordato, a handsome man who talked politics with Percy and taught Greek to Mary. "Do you not envy my luck that, having begun Greek, an amiable, young, agreeable, and learned Greek Prince comes every morning to give me a lesson of an hour and a half?" Mary wrote to her friend Mrs. Gisborne. Mavrocordato would play a role later in persuading Byron to join the rebellion in which he lost his life.

Page 82: Shelley always underestimated the dangers of the sea. When Trelawny suggested they hire a more experienced fisherman to help them on the crew, Shelley proudly insisted he could steer the boat with one hand and read a book by the philosopher Plato with the other!

Page 85: The keeping and preserving of the body parts of loved ones or of great people was a common practice of the 1800s. Many such relics of famed people are kept in museums and private collections to this day.

Page 120: Although Mary refused to cooperate with Trelawny on his memoirs about Shelley and Byron, he did publish his book seven years after Mary's death. It was titled *The Recollections of the Last Days of Shelley and Byron*.

Page 106: Claire retired in 1870 at the age of 72. She became a Roman Catholic and entered a convent in Florence. She died there in 1879, having become quite bitter over what she considered the mistakes of her youth. The newspapers made scant notice of her passing.

Timeline

1797   Mary Wollstonecraft Godwin born on August 29. Mary
        Wollstonecrat dies less than two weeks afterward.
1801   William Godwin marries Mary Jane Clairmont.
1814   On July 28, Mary and Percy Shelley, elope to the Continent.
1815   Mary's first child, a daughter, is born in January, and
        lives less than two weeks.
1816   A son, William, is born in January. In May, Mary,
        Percy, Claire, and Byron leave for Italy, where Mary begins
        writing *Frankenstein*. Fanny Imlay, Mary's half-sister commits
        suicide in October. Harriet Westbrook Shelley, Percy's first wife,
        commits suicide in December.
1817   Mary and Percy's daughter Clara is born in September.
1818   *Frankenstein* published in March as Mary and Percy
        leave for Italy. Clara dies in September.
1819   William dies in June. Mary's last child, Percy Florence,
        is born in November.
1822   Allegra dies in April. In July, Percy and Edward Williams drown
        while sailing.
1823   Mary and Percy Florence return to England. *Valperga* published.
1824   Lord Byron dies.
1826   *The Last Man* published.
1830   *Perkin Warbeck* published.
1835   *Lodore* published.
1836   William Godwin dies.
1837   *Falkner* published.
1840   *History of a Six Weeks Tour* published. Mary travels to
        the Continent with Percy Florence and friends.
1844   *Rambles in German and Italy* published.
1848   Percy Florence marries Jane St. John.
1851   Mary Shelley dies in London and is buried in
        Bournemouth churchyard.

Major Works of Mary Shelley

Frankenstein; or, The Modern Promethus. London: Henry Colburn and Richard Bentley, 1831. (One volume edition.)

Valperga: Or, the Life and Adventures of Castruccio, Prince of Lucca. London: G. and W.B. Whittaker, 1823.

The Last Man. London: Henry Colburn, 1826.

The Fortunes of Perkin Warbeck, A Romance. London: Henry Colburn and Richard Bentley, 1830.

Lodore. London: Ric hard Bentley, 1835.

Falkner. London: Saunders and Otley, 1837.

Charles E. Robinson, ed., *Mary Shelley: Collected Tales and Stories.* Baltimore and London: The Johns Hopkins University Press, 1976.

Sources

The Mother Gone Before

p.12   "She shall be nobody's little girl . . ." C. Kegan Paul, *William Godwin: His Friends and Contemporaries* (AMS Press, New York, 1970), Vol. 1, 365.

p.14   ". . . the only offspring . . ." Emily W. Sunstein, *Mary Shelley: Romance and Reality* (Little, Brown and Company, Boston, 1989) 23.

p.19   "My own daughter . . ." Paul, Vol. II, 214.

Mad Shelley

p.25   "A thrilling voice . . ." Thomas Jefferson Hogg, T*he Life of Percy Bysshe Shelley* (Edward Moxn, London, 1858), 537-538.

p.26   "I have pledged myself . . ."Sunstein, 76.

p.28   "They wish to separate . . ." Richard Holmes, *Shelley: The Pursuit* (Weidenfeld and Nicholson, London, 1974), 233.

Romance

p.30   "How dreadful did . . ." Paula R. Feldman and Diana Scott Kilvert, eds., *The Journals of Mary Shelley* (The Clarendon Press, Oxford, 1987), Vol.I, 6.

p.31   "Mary, look . . ." Feldman and Kilvert, 7.

p.31   "It was acting a novel . . ." Sunstein, 83.

p.31   "Oh, dear, no! . . ." Marion Kingston Stocking, ed., *The Journals of Claire Clairmont* (Harvard University Press, Cambridge, Mass, 1968), 31.

p.33   "Let me observe . . .) Feldman and Kilvert, 12.

p.34   "Determined at last . . ." Feldman and Kilvert, 19.

p.34   "Twere easier for . . ." Feldman and Kilvert, 21.

Return to Reality

p.37   "The next morning . . ." Feldman and Kilvert, 37.

p.38   "Every church in . . ." Feldman and Kilvert, 50.

p.39   ". . . think of my . . ." Feldman and Kilvert, 69.

p.39   "Dream that my . . ." Feldman and Kilvert, 70.

p.41   "In my judgement . . ." Frederick L. Jones, ed., *The Letters of Percy Bysshe Shelley* (The Clarendon Press, Oxford, 1964) Vol.I, 459.

p.45   "How mild he is! . . ." Sunstein, 37.

The Monster's Tale

p.47   "Sometimes the road . . ." Frederick L. Jones, *The Letters of Mary Wollstonecraft Shelley* (University of Oklahoma Press, Norman, Oklahoma, 1944), Vol. I, 9-11.

p.48   "I feel happy . . ." Jones, MWS, Vol.I, 11.

p.51   "We will each write . . ." Sunstein, 121.

p.53   "I saw the hideous . . ." Mary Shelley, *Frankenstein, or the Modern Promethus* (Henry Colburn and Richard Bentley, London, 1831), ix-x.

p.54   "I have found it." Shelley, xi.

p.59   "Invention, it must be . . ." Shelley, xi.

Suicides

p.61   "You often deceive . . ." Muriel Spark, *Child of Light: A Reassessment of Mary Wollstonecraft Shelley* (Tower Bridge Publications, Hadleigh/Essex, Great Britian, 1951), 47-48.

p.62   "I depart immediately . . ." Eileen Bigland, *Mary Shelley* (Appleton-Century-Crofts, Inc., New York, 1959), 103.

p.63   "I did indeed . . ." Bigland, 55.

p.64   "A respectable woman . . ." Holmes, 352.

p.64   "According to the vulgar . . ." Spark, 51.

p.65   "I now have . . ."Bigland, 111-112.

p.65   "I have not . . ." Jones, *PBS*, Vol. I, 517.

p.66   "No words can . . ." Spark, 52-53.

p.68   "You tell me . . . " Jones, *MWS*, Vol.I, 41-42.

Little Deaths

p.70   "It is strange . . ." Jones, *MWS*, Vol.I, 52.

p.70   "We have no idea . . ." Jones, Vol.I, 49.

p.72   "You should . . . recognize . . ." Spark, 58.

p.73   "To see the sun . . ." Bigland, 137.

p.74   "His health and strength . . ." Bigland, 143.

p.74   "William is in . . ." Jones, *MWS*, Vol.I, 72-73.

p.75   "Yesterday, after an illness . . ." Jones, *PBS*, Vol.II, 97.

p.76   "Begun July 21st . . ." Bigland, 146.

The Man Behind Shelley
p.81   "In the middle . . ." Bigland, 199.
p.84   "How are you . . ." Jones, *PBS*, Vol.II, 444.
p.85   "Shelley, the writer . . ." Holmes, 730.
p.86   "You are free . . ." Feldman and Kilvert, Vol.II, 436.
p.86   "I never saw . . ." Sunstein, 223.
p.86   "Well, here is . . ." Jones, *MWS*, Vol.I., 179-180.
False Hearts
p.89   "But lo, and behold . . ." Jones, *MWS*, Vol.I, 259.
p.91   "Shelley has celebrity . . ." Spark, 90.
p.91   "My imagination is dead . . ." Feldman and Kilvert, Vol.II, 474.
p.92   "Mary Shelley shall be written . . ." Sunstein, 312.
p.92   "I was more delighted . . . Spark, 103.
p.92   ". . . that resplendent spirit . . ." Feldman and Kilvert, Vol.II, 479.
p.93   "He could hardly . . ." Jones, *MWS*, Vol.I, 298.
p.94   "I feel my powers . . ." Feldman and Kilvert, Vol.II, 479.
p.94   "Thank God, it is over!" Spark, 92.
"Proof Against Man & Woman"
p.95   "I am copying . . ." Bigland, 83.
p.97   "It was rather dull. . ." Spark, 100.
p.98   "I should not wonder . . ." Spark, 102.
p.99   "Poor Perkin Warbeck." Spark, 101.
p.100   "To go and live . . ." Jones, *MWS*, Vol.II, 72.
p.100   "I am now proof . . ." Spark, 88.
Words in Stone
p.101   "His last moments . . ." Jones, *MWS*, Vol.II, 114.
p.102   "My race is run." Feldman and Kilvert, Vol.II, 546.
p.102   "lovely from her birth. Sunstein, 333.
p.104   "I much disliked . . ." Feldman and Kilvert, Vol.II, 560.
p.105   "There . . . stood Diodati . . ." Bigland, 263-264.
p.105   ". . . falling from the stalk . . ." Spark, 115.
p.106   "She is a prize . . ." Spark, 119.
p.106   "She has been . . ." Spark, 119.
p.107   "I shall join . . ." Noel Gerson, *Daughter of Earth and Water: A Biography of Mary Wollstonecraft Shelly* (William Morrow & Co. New York, 1973), 269.
p.107   "It would have broken . . ." Sunstein, 384.
p.108   "God and good angels . . ." Feldman and Kilvert, Vol.II, 565.

Bibliography

Brian W. Aldiss. *Billion Year Spree: The True History of Science Fiction*. New York: Schocken Books, 1974.

Eileen Bigland. *Mary Shelley*. New York: Appleton-Century-Crofts, Inc., 1959.

Ford K. Brown. *The Life of William Godwin*. New York: : E.P. Dutton & Co., 1926. (Reprint: Folcroft, Pa.: Folcroft Library Editions.)

Louise Shutz Boas. *Harriet Shelley: Five Long Years*. London: Oxford University Press, 1962.

Jane Dunn. *Moon in Eclipse: A Life of Mary Shelley*. London: Weidenfeld & Nicolson, 1978.

Paula R. Feldman, Diana Scott-Kilvert, eds. *The Journals of Mary Shelley, 1814-1844, Vols. I, II*. Oxford: Oxford University Press, 1987.

Noel B. Gerson. *Daughter of Earth and Water: A Biography of Mary Wollstonecraft Shelley*. New York: William Morrow & Company, Inc., 1973.

Robert Gittings. *Claire Clairmont and the Shelleys, 1798-1879*. New York: Oxford Univeristy Press, 1992.

Janet Harris. *The Woman Who Created Frankenstein: A Portrait of Mary Shelley*. New York: Harper & Row, 1979.

Thomas Jefferson Hogg. *The Life of Percy Bysshe Shelley*. London: Edward Moxn, 1858.

Richard Holmes. *Shelley: The Pursuit*. New York: E.P. Dutton & Co., Inc, 1975.

Frederick L. Jones, ed. *The Letters of Mary W. Shelley, Vols. I, II.* Norman, Oklahoma: University of Oklahoma Press, 1944.

————. *The Letters of Percy Bysshe Shelley.* Oxford: The Clarendon Press, 1964.

W.H. Lyles. *Mary Shelley: An Annotated Bibliography.* New York and London: Garland Publishing, 1975.

Elizabeth Nitchie. *Mary Shelley: Author of Frankenstein.* New Brunswick, New Jersey, 1953.

C. Kegan Paul. *William Godwin: His Friends and Contemporaries.* New York: AMS Press, 1970.

Frederick Raphael. *Byron.* New York: Thames and Hudson, Inc., 1982.

Mary Shelley. *Frankenstein, or the Modern Promethus,* 2nd Edition. London: Henry Colburn and Richard Bentley, 1831.

Christopher Small. *Mary Shelley's Frankenstein: Tracing the Myth.* Pittsburgh, Pa: University of Pittsburgh Press, 1973.

Muriel Spark. *Child of Light: A Reassessment of Mary Wollstonecraft Shelley.* Hadleigh/Essex, Great Britian, 1951.

Marion Kingston Stocking. *The Clairmont Correspondence: Letters of Claire Clairmont, Charles Clairmont, and Fanny Imlay Godwin, Vol.I, 1808-1834.* Baltimore, Md: The Johns Hopkins University Press, 1985.

————. *The Journals of Claire Clairmont.* Cambridge, Ma: Harvard University Press, 1968.

Emily W. Sunstein. *Mary Shelley: Romance and Reality.* Boston:, Brown and Company, 1989.

Index

PHOTO CREDITS